Student Choices

Series Editor: Cara Acred

Volume 264

Independence Educational Publishers

First published by Independence Educational Publishers

The Studio, High Green

Great Shelford

Cambridge CB22 5EG

England

© Independence 2014

Copyright

Photocopy licence

British Library Cataloguing in Publication Data

Student choices. -- (Issues ; 264)
1. Education, Higher--Great Britain. 2. Education,
Higher--Standards--Great Britain. 3. Higher education and
state--Great Britain.
I. Series II. Acred, Cara editor.
378.4'1-dc23

ISBN-13: 9781861686794

Printed in Great Britain

MWL Print Group Ltd

Contents

Introduction

Student Choices is Volume 264 in the **ISSUES** series. The aim of the series is to offer current, diverse information about important issues in our world, from a UK perspective.

ABOUT STUDENT CHOICES

Today's students are faced with increasingly difficult decisions. With tuition fees at their highest and graduate jobs hard to come by, many young people are questioning whether University is the right choice. This book explores the alternatives to University, such as apprenticeships and career colleges. It also considers the outlook for those who do attend University – examining how they might deal with stress, debt and budgeting. In the final chapter, articles focus on the outlook for graduates in today's labour market.

OUR SOURCES

Titles in the **ISSUES** series are designed to function as educational resource books, providing a balanced overview of a specific subject.

The information in our books is comprised of facts, articles and opinions from many different sources, including:

⇨ Newspaper reports and opinion pieces

⇨ Website factsheets

⇨ Magazine and journal articles

⇨ Statistics and surveys

⇨ Government reports

⇨ Literature from special interest groups

A NOTE ON CRITICAL EVALUATION

Because the information reprinted here is from a number of different sources, readers should bear in mind the origin of the text and whether the source is likely to have a particular bias when presenting information (or when conducting their research). It is hoped that, as you read about the many aspects of the issues explored in this book, you will critically evaluate the information presented.

It is important that you decide whether you are being presented with facts or opinions. Does the writer give a biased or unbiased report? If an opinion is being expressed, do you agree with the writer? Is there potential bias to the 'facts' or statistics behind an article?

ASSIGNMENTS

In the back of this book, you will find a selection of assignments designed to help you engage with the articles you have been reading and to explore your own opinions. Some tasks will take longer than others and there is a mixture of design, writing and research based activities that you can complete alone or in a group.

FURTHER RESEARCH

At the end of each article we have listed its source and a website that you can visit if you would like to conduct your own research. Please remember to critically evaluate any sources that you consult and consider whether the information you are viewing is accurate and unbiased.

Useful weblinks

www.accommodationforstudents.com

www.agcas.org.uk

www.allaboutschoolleavers.co.uk

www.barnardos.org.uk

www.careercolleges.org.uk

www.graduateadvantage.co.uk

www.hefce.ac.uk

www.nus.org.uk

www.theconversation.com

www.themoneycharity.org.uk

www.thestudentpocketguide.com

www.ucas.com

www.youthsight.com

What can I do with my A-levels?

University, university, university. That's the only reason why you do A-levels, right? Well, it's a fantastic option, but A-levels aren't just a one-way ticket to university. It's high time that we start acknowledging ALL the options A-levels open up. So kick back and relax as we take you through a whirlwind tour of what you can do with your A-levels.

Option 1: University

It's the traditional route and still a very good one. Degrees are not to be sniffed at and can be the ticket to some great career options. If you're set on going to university, you'll need to do plenty of research into the degree courses and universities on offer, finding one that tallies with your interests and career plans. You can browse our university profiles and courses section to find out more. Tuition fees might seem like a lot, but there is plenty of financial support out there in the form of loans, bursaries and grants that you can take advantage of.

The long university holidays can be used to build up work experience, or you can opt for a sandwich degree course that involves a year spent working in industry. Degrees are great if you want to keep your career options open, access certain careers that are only open to graduates, or if you simply want to study a subject that you are passionate about. On average, graduates tend to get higher starting salaries and earn more over their lifetime.

However, university isn't for everyone. Some people want to get stuck straight into work or are put off by the cost of university. There are other options where you can work for a company, whilst gaining a degree.

Option 2: Sponsored degree programme

If you want to go to university but are daunted by the cost, sponsored degree programmes might be just the ticket. Sponsored degree programmes come in all shapes and sizes. For example, there are ones where you'll attend university part-time whilst working for the company that foots your tuition fees.

'If you want to leap straight into the world of work but still want to gain some serious qualifications, then a school leaver programme might be the thing for you'

Other sponsored degree programmes allow school leavers to study a course full-time at university, which has been devised by a consortium of employers or a single company in conjunction with the host institution.

On the plus side, sponsored degree programmes can offer you some much needed financial assistance to help fund your way through university. Particularly for those with work experience as part of the programme, they can help you build up a relationship with an employer and enhance your employment prospects after university.

Seems like a no brainer then? Well, sponsored degree programmes aren't all sunshine and rainbows. They suffer from a lack of choice, only being available at a limited number of universities and covering a limited range of degree courses and career paths.

Option 3: Gap year

You don't have to dive straight into university or permanent employment. If you're a bit bewildered about your options, or just fancy some breathing space, a gap year might be right for you.

It's not just a year to kick back and do nothing, though; you won't really impress many people doing that. Most people work for a bit and then go travelling. Many of the large companies, such as KPMG, Bank of England

and IBM have gap year programmes for those wishing to get in a solid year of work experience. Alternatively, you might want to volunteer in the UK or abroad, or use your time off to get plenty of work experience. This may even help you figure out which careers might interest you.

The key thing, if you do decide to do a gap year, is to make sure you do something worthwhile. Some universities and employers won't look favourably on gap years where you've just spent your entire time in the clubs of South America. Try and make sure you've included some more valuable experiences in your gap year, as well as partying.

Option 4: School leaver programme

If you want to leap straight into the world of work but still want to gain some serious qualifications, then a school leaver programme might be the thing for you. These schemes usually involve studying for a degree or professional qualification, whilst working for a company. As an employee, you'll get a wage and they'll cover your training costs. That means you can earn while you learn and avoid student debt.

School leaver programmes are designed to offer a genuine alternative to university. Entry onto a scheme can be very competitive. The big finance and accountancy firms dominate the school leaver programme market at the moment, but other opportunities can be found in industries like engineering, IT, retail, digital media and hospitality. Bear in mind, school leaver programmes are still relatively new and therefore aren't common in most industries.

Option 5: Higher Apprenticeship

There is something else you can do with those A-levels, and that's a Higher Apprenticeship. These are the crème de la crème of apprenticeships. Higher Apprenticeships bear many similarities to school leaver programmes (in fact, many school leaver programmes include a Higher Apprenticeship as part of their training programme) but tend to be shorter.

You can also get qualifications like foundation degrees, HNDs and undergraduate degrees as part of a Higher Apprenticeship. Apprentices can usually top up their qualifications after the apprenticeship too.

Of course, some people bypass all of these options and plunge straight into employment. It's up to you to have a good think, do some research and work out the best option for you. Don't just think about the short term. Try and imagine where you want to be in five or ten years, and figure out the best way to get there.

Deciding what to do after A-levels is one of the biggest decisions you'll make, so choose wisely!

⇨ The above information is reprinted with kind permission from AllAboutSchoolLeavers.co.uk. Please visit their website for further information.

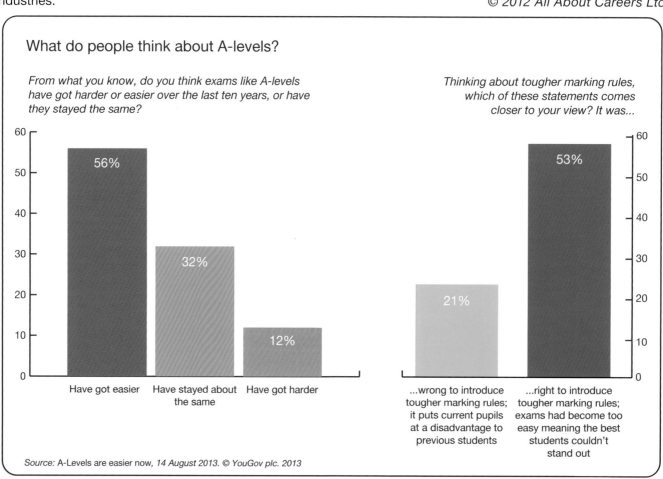

What do people think about A-levels?

From what you know, do you think exams like A-levels have got harder or easier over the last ten years, or have they stayed the same?

Thinking about tougher marking rules, which of these statements comes closer to your view? It was...

- 56% — Have got easier
- 32% — Have stayed about the same
- 12% — Have got harder

- 21% — ...wrong to introduce tougher marking rules; it puts current pupils at a disadvantage to previous students
- 53% — ...right to introduce tougher marking rules; exams had become too easy meaning the best students couldn't stand out

Source: A-Levels are easier now, 14 August 2013. © YouGov plc. 2013

A-level results: what to do if your grades aren't enough

A-level results day always seems to be filled with news reports and articles on happy students in their school hall beaming away with their straight A results transcripts, right? Or doing one of those 'jump for joy' poses in the air? And that rather irritating comment that exams are getting easier tends to crop up too. Have they tried A-level maths recently?!

18-year-olds across the country have spent weeks worrying about their future destinations. There's a lot of pressure riding on that one piece of paper! So when the day finally arrives and you are one of those jolly souls to have bagged the right grades for what you want to do next and where you want to go, that's definitely a licence to party!

But what about the rest of us?

A-level results aren't always the most pleasant of experiences for everyone. There are still plenty of people out there who don't quite manage to get the grades they need for their plans. And if you're one of them, it can feel worse than that envelope moment for the losing contender on *Britain's Got Talent*, *The Voice* and *X Factor* combined. Understatement, much?

When you've worked so hard for two years and just missed out on your goal it's tough. And it's okay to be disappointed. But all will not be lost! So you need an action plan to prepare you for that bit of paper and what to do if things don't quite go to plan on A-level results day…

So what do you do if your A-level grades aren't enough?

'My life is over!!' Err, think again! If you don't quite get what you need for Plan A, this does NOT mean that you are useless, no good and won't ever get an education, job or career. So first things first, get that out of your head right away! We mean it. Just talk to some of the people around you: we guarantee you'll find someone who didn't quite get the grades, and they're still standing!

If your plan was to go to university and your heart's still set on this, then keep calm and call the exam results helpline. Advisors are available throughout the exam results period to discuss what you can do with lower, or even higher grades than expected. It'll be really busy on A-level results day, so perhaps giving them a call beforehand might not be a bad idea, just to get your head straight about your potential options.

Clearing can be a stressful process if you are still sure you want to go to university. The best way to deal with it is to be very focused about the course you want to study, and ensure you select the best course available to you for that subject area.

Sponsored degrees

If a traditional university route isn't an option with your results, you might be able to try another way in: sponsored degrees. Some big companies will now pay for successful applicants with A-level qualifications to study a full degree at university, whilst also gaining work experience and training in their offices. The scheme then leads to a job with the company once you've got your degree. One way to avoid tuition fees!

Higher Apprenticeships

If your grades aren't what you expect, you may still be a perfect candidate for an Intermediate Apprenticeship or a Higher Apprenticeship.

Modern apprenticeships are kind of a big deal. They are offered by some of the biggest graduate employers in the UK, such as PwC, Deloitte, National Grid and Visa Europe, provide structured training and pay competitive salaries. Newsflash: You don't need a degree to pursue a career as an engineer, accountant, I.T. specialist or even a lawyer nowadays!

Higher Apprenticeships require applicants to have A-levels, sometimes in relevant subjects to the type of career, so numerically-based qualifications will be good for an accountancy apprenticeship, for example.

You could also apply for a job straight away. However, you may be less likely to gain as much formal structured training. On completing a Higher Apprenticeship, which can last up to five years, you will be at the same level as any graduate, with even more on-the-job experience. Some even result in a permanent job at the company you've been an apprentice for. It paves a route for serious progression within the chosen sector. Hello employability!

More and more companies are seeing the importance of employing bright, keen young people to start learning the ropes in an apprenticeship format, and the Government is pressing for the creation of more of these options in the near future. So having a dip into some more information about apprenticeships as a back-up plan, or even first choice, isn't such a shabby idea!

Talk about it!

Whatever you decide, don't bottle up your frustrations regarding your results and your next move. Family, friends, school careers advisors and teachers are there to help you through. It's important to know there ARE options out there for you. AllAboutSchoolLeavers and AllAboutCareers has plenty of information about jobs and career paths for school leavers.

Places for university may be becoming more competitive, but there is certainly an option out there for everyone – even if they don't get the results they expect. And there is most definitely life after A-level results!

⇨ The above information is reprinted with kind permission from AllAboutSchoolLeavers. co.uk. Please visit their website for further information.

Careers guidance services are failing young people

The Government risks replacing face-to-face careers guidance with remote online schemes that young people report they can't use or don't even know exist, jeopardising their chances of getting sustainable work, Barnardo's research reveals today.

Last year, the Government transferred responsibility for delivering careers guidance away from local authorities, and passed it on to schools and a mixture of web and phone-based services instead. Remote services include the flagship National Careers Service (NCS) website and helpline for all ages, expected to reach 370,000 young people per year, and the Plotr site for 11–25-year-olds.

However, Barnardo's *Helping the inbetweeners* report on the state of England's careers provision, reveals that these services are not reaching young people – especially those 'in between', who may have low qualifications and be disengaged from school but don't qualify for extra support because they're not classified as the most 'at risk' by local authorities.

Not one young person Barnardo's interviewed for the research reported that they knew that the NCS website or the Government-funded Plotr site existed.

Meanwhile, the nominally 'free' national careers service helpline in fact costs up to 40p per minute to call from a mobile – making it virtually unaffordable for the many young people who don't have access to landlines. The national NCS phone line should be made free from all mobiles so that young people can get good quality advice and guidance.

The report also explores the impact of transferring formerly local authority run face-to-face services, such as Connexions, onto schools. It finds some young people reporting that their school provided few face-to-face sessions and, in some cases, no one-to-one sessions. Disengaged pupils reported that they'd missed sessions or felt unable to trust the careers guidance given by schools, as they assumed the advice would be prejudiced.

Barnardo's is calling on the Government to:

⇨ Make the national NCS phone line number free from all mobiles

⇨ Ensure NCS number is Skype-accessible so callers can access face-to-face guidance

⇨ Revamp online careers guidance services so they are higher quality and better promoted amongst young people

⇨ Guarantee face-to-face careers guidance for all young people who ask for it.

Barnardo's Assistant Director of Policy, Jonathan Rallings, comments:

'Changes to our careers guidance system risk squandering young futures by failing to guarantee sufficient vital face-to-face support for people who need it.

'The near-total lack of awareness amongst the young people interviewed about the Government's website and helpline means that they are effectively offering "ghost" services in the place of meaningful advice.

'It's crucial that the Government doesn't miss the opportunity to step in at this pivotal age, especially when access to trusted, personally tailored careers advice at an early stage can help to make the difference between young people sinking or swimming in the world of work.'

27 August 2013

⇨ The above information is reprinted with kind permission from Barnardo's. Please visit www.barnardos.org.uk for further information.

Study finds mentoring key to influencing pupils to apply to university

Appropriately-timed student mentoring schemes can have a large and substantiate effect on influencing secondary pupils from disadvantaged areas apply to university. These are the findings of a pilot study, published today, that tested the impact and delivery of mentoring on pupils' intentions to apply to university.

The Economic and Social Research Council [ESRC]-funded experiment, conducted in a Bristol secondary state school over a single morning and timed to coincide after a session given to pupils on personal statements, comprised a series of short presentations by trained mentors about university life.

Four mentors, who are second and third-year students at the University of Bristol, gave the same talk to 53 Year 12 students (aged between 16 and 18) who had been randomly allocated to four groups, which varied as to the type of mentoring the pupils received and the timing at which some questions were answered.

Before and after each talk, students were also asked to complete a survey that asked them questions about their aspirations, including whether any of their close family members or friends attended university, and indicate (on a scale of one to ten) how likely they were apply to a university or the University of Bristol.

Survey data showed that students asked to estimate how likely they were to attend university, after receiving the mentoring stated they were 19 per cent more likely to apply to university than when they were asked to make the same estimation before. Results showed no difference in the groups that had a longer mentoring talk with shorter questions or vice versa.

Michael Sanders, the study's lead author and a PhD student in the University's Centre for Market and Public Organisation, said: 'Despite attempts to increase rates of university enrolment from disadvantaged backgrounds, statistically these people are still less likely to attend university and if they do apply, they apply to less prestigious universities.

'Although further study is needed to determine the longer-term effects, these findings show that an appropriately-timed inspirational young person talking about university education is sufficient to encourage others. Most importantly, even if the effects of this mentoring are short-lived, this time of a young person's life may represent a "teachable moment" at which their behaviour can be positively influenced by a low-cost intervention that can have a positive and significant effect.

'Student mentoring programmes, such as the one trialled in this paper need not necessarily be primarily concerned with increasing academic attainment, but rather aspiration and understanding by poorer students that "people like me" can attend excellent academic institutions.'

Further information:

ESRC

The study entitled *Aspiration & Inspiration - A pilot study of mentoring in schools* by Michael Sanders (1), Ariella Kristal (2), Farooq Sabri (1), Alex Tupper (1) is published by the University of Bristol's Centre for Market and Public Organisation.

1. University of Bristol, Centre for Market and Public Organisation (CMPO), Bristol, UK.

2. Yale University, New Haven, Connecticut, USA.

ESRC

The Economic and Social Research Council (ESRC) is the UK's largest organisation for funding research on economic and social issues. It supports independent, high-quality research which has an impact on business, the public sector and the third sector. The ESRC's total budget for 2012/13 is £205 million. At any one time the ESRC supports over 4,000 researchers and postgraduate students in academic institutions and independent research institutes. More at www.esrc.ac.uk.

11 October 2013

⇨ The above information is reprinted with kind permission from the University of Bristol. Please visit www.bris.ac.uk for further information.

'Learn as you earn' courses – some of the best

Examples of innovative delivery partnerships.

Business-designed courses

Universities, colleges and businesses work together to design programmes.

Hewlett Packard has entered into strategic partnerships with universities including Staffordshire University, Buckinghamshire New University, Coventry University, the University of the West of England and De Montfort University.

These universities have integrated HP Institute into their curriculum and they work with HP to provide mentoring and guest lectures, internships for students and other collaborative ventures. HP will continue to seek new university partnerships.

Based at the University of Warwick, WMG collaborates with global companies including Astra Zeneca, IBM, Jaguar Land Rover, Rolls-Royce, Tata Motors European Technical Centre (TMTEC) and TVS Motor Company to develop collaborative research and taught programmes.

The New College Nottingham Academy of Construction is the largest provider of construction training in the East Midlands. Industry representatives, including the Nottingham Construction Forum, are proactively involved in the design of provision and focus of the college's construction portfolio to ensure alignment with local industry need.

School leaver programmes

Employers hire school leavers at 18 and train them on a tailored degree course. School leavers are employees from day one and spend part of their time in the workplace.

KPMG has partnered with Durham, Exeter and Birmingham Universities to offer a six-year training contract that includes a relevant university honours degree and a professional accountancy qualification.

Throughout the programme, students receive an annual salary and have all their tuition fees and university accommodation costs paid by KPMG.

The Rolls-Royce A-Level entry programme is designed to develop the next generation of manufacturing specialists and leads to a Master's degree from the University of Warwick.

Alongside part-time university study, students undertake a series of mentored placements in areas such as forecasting and production planning.

Advanced and Higher Apprenticeships

Work-based training programmes, designed around the needs of employers that lead to Level 3 and Level 4+ vocational qualifications. Time is split between theoretical and practical, work-based learning.

PWC led a group of 40 employers in the professional services sector to design the content of the new Professional Services Higher Apprenticeship (PSHA), with pathways in audit, tax and consulting at level 4. A follow-on Higher Apprenticeship at level 7 became available earlier this year.

British Airways has partnered with QA to develop a two-and-a-half-year Higher Apprenticeship in project management. Leading to a Level 4 Diploma, the apprenticeship combines formal training with practical work experience and mentoring.

Co-operative models are also being developed by firms – Toyota in Derbyshire has preserved and developed capacity at its Apprentice Development Centre by working in partnership with providers to extend provision to suppliers and local businesses.

Work-based learning programmes

Jointly designed, tailored university programmes, delivered either part-time or full-time for full-time employees, incorporating day-to-day workplace practices.

McDonald's has partnered with Manchester Metropolitan University to develop and accredit the retailer's Foundation Degree programme for restaurant managers.

Anglia Ruskin University partners with many organisations, which have included Ridgeons, the RAF, Harrods and Willmott Dixon to provide work-based learning programmes.

For example, working with East Anglia-based builders' merchant Ridgeons to develop a fast-track Foundation Degree which enables staff to build key management skills. Students study and work full time throughout the course.

Hull College is among a number of further education colleges that provide tailored work-based learning programmes for employers. It has worked with employers including P&O, BAE, TNT and BP to deliver bespoke training programmes at Levels 3 and 4.

⇨ The above information is reprinted with kind permission from The CBI. Please visit www.cbi.org.uk for further information.

What is a Career College?

Career Colleges will increase the range and choice of opportunities open to 14–19-year-olds. They will provide accelerated vocationally-focused programmes of study at colleges equipped to the highest standards and staffed by expert teachers, supported by employers.

They will:

⇨ Be established by Further Education (FE) colleges

⇨ Specialise in subjects linked directly to sectors with exceptional job prospects

⇨ Partner with employers to design and deliver the curriculum and work experience

⇨ Ensure employers represent a minimum of 40% of career college board members

⇨ Offer 14 to 19 provision, with progression to apprenticeships, higher education and employment

⇨ Against a background of high youth unemployment, the over-arching target is that every young person leaving a Career College, whether at 16 or 18, will be in work, training or education.

How do they differ from a regular FE college?

Career Colleges will offer practical training and education designed by industry, with direct input from employers to the training of young people. They are specialist training centres, offered in areas with real prospects of employment, driven by the market.

They differ from a regular FE college by being a 'college within a college'. They will have access to specialist teachers and facilities, but because student numbers will be limited, each Career College will create its own identity.

Why are they important? Why do we need them?

The skills gap is evident in the UK and there are high levels of youth unemployment. People with outstanding vocational and practical abilities are vital to our economy.

The Government has already put in place reforms to ensure that students can combine core academic subjects with high-quality vocational qualifications from age 14. And at 16, two thirds of students in full-time education take some kind of vocational subject

By specialising in a vocational area relevant to the local labour market, Career Colleges will help engage employers and give young people the chance to start a high-quality level 2 vocational course at 14. If they choose to stay in that vocational area, they will then be ready to progress to a higher level of vocational learning at 16. This could put them ahead by a whole two years.

In addition, Career College students will learn through real-world challenges set and supported by employers. Coupled with work experience – both pre- and post-16 – and other links with local businesses, they will develop the wider employability skills which employers rate so highly.

Combining academic and vocational studies in this way has been proven to work. It's the popular choice for huge numbers of young people in Austria, Switzerland and Germany – and as a result, their youth unemployment is far lower than almost anywhere in the world, including England. It's easy to see why.

Career Colleges are set in the context of a further education sector which is able to respond to local needs by determining the right offer and the most appropriate delivery model to meet those needs.

When will Career Colleges be open and how many will there be?

The first Career College will open in September 2014. The ambition is to open 40 Career Colleges in the next four years, driven by market needs, not individual interest.

Who decides on the curriculum? Can they specialise in ANY subject?

The curriculum will be driven by requirements for progression to higher education and employment, with great influence and direction from employers in the relevant sector they serve. As Career Colleges are demand-driven, their subjects will be determined by need and opportunities for young people, ensuring adherence to national requirements for 14-to-19 education.

How will the Career Colleges be scrutinised?

Career Colleges will be subject to the same scrutiny and benchmarking as FE colleges across the UK, with opportunities to compare learner successes with all other provision in the UK. We are currently exploring international measures to scrutinise standards and ensure we continue to aspire to provide the best education and work opportunities for young people. A key measure of performance for Career Colleges will be the number of young people who secure work and further and higher education, directly following their education in a Career College.

⇨ The above information is reprinted with kind permission from the Career Colleges Trust. Please visit www.careercolleges.org.uk.

© Career Colleges Trust 2014

Apprenticeships

1. Applications and qualifications

Apply for an apprenticeship

Anyone in England can apply for an apprenticeship if they're:

⇨ 16 or over

⇨ eligible to work in England

⇨ not in full-time education.

First search for a vacancy on the Apprenticeships website, then register on the site and apply.

Apprenticeships take between one and four years to complete depending on their level.

Work and study

Apprenticeships combine practical training in a job with study.

An apprentice:

⇨ works alongside experienced staff

⇨ gains job-specific skills

⇨ earns a wage

⇨ studies towards a related qualification (usually one day a week).

Levels of apprenticeship

There are three levels in England:

⇨ Intermediate – equivalent to five GCSE passes

⇨ Advanced – equivalent to two A-level passes

⇨ Higher – lead to NVQ Level 4 and above or a Foundation Degree.

Qualifications

Apprenticeships can lead to:

⇨ National Vocational Qualifications (NVQs) at Level 2, 3, 4 or 5

⇨ Functional Skills qualifications, e.g. in maths, English or ICT

⇨ a technical certificate, such as a BTEC or City & Guilds Progression Award

⇨ knowledge-based qualifications, such as a Higher National Certificate (HNC), a Higher National Diploma (HND) or a foundation degree.

2. Pay and holidays

Pay and right to minimum wage

Apprentices are paid from the first day of their apprenticeship and they're entitled to the National Minimum Wage.

The current minimum wage rate for an apprentice is £2.68 per hour. This rate applies to apprentices aged 16 to 18 and those aged 19 or over who are in their first year.

Apprentices aged 19 or over who have completed their first year must be paid at least the minimum wage rate for their age.

Hours apprentices are paid for

Apprentices must be paid for:

⇨ their normal working hours (minimum 30 hours per week)

⇨ training that is part of the apprenticeship (usually one day per week).

Example

Tim is an apprentice aged 17 and works 35 hours per week including 1 day of training.

Apprentice rate: £2.68 per hour x 35

Total Tim gets paid per week: £93.80

Holidays

Apprentices get at least 20 days of paid holiday per year, plus bank holidays.

Help and advice

Apprentices can contact the Pay and Work Rights Helpline for free and confidential advice on their rights at work.

⇨ The above information is reprinted with kind permission from GOV.UK.

Apprenticeship vs university

We think university is great. It can open up a world of possibilities, allow you to explore a subject you're passionate about and give you access to a whole range of careers. Equally, as you can guess, we're pretty passionate about apprenticeships. They give you the chance to head straight into work, whilst picking up qualifications and receiving a wage.

It's not that one is better than the other; you just need to figure out which route is the most suited to you. That's why we'd hesitate to make grand sweeping claims about how apprenticeships are better than university or vice versa. What we can do is help you weigh up your choices.

So how do you choose between the two?

OK, so let's do a little myth-busting and sweep those cobwebs of misconception away. First of all, choosing the apprenticeship route doesn't mean that you are turning your back on a university education. Apprentices can still go to university and study for higher qualifications. A Higher Apprenticeship, for instance, allows you to gain a Level 4 or above qualification, e.g. a foundation degree, HND, HNC or undergraduate degree. After the apprenticeship, things like foundation degrees, HND and HNCs can be topped up to a full honours bachelor's degree.

Neither are apprenticeships solely for those who 'don't have the grades' to go to university. There are some challenging apprenticeship schemes out there, with tough application processes and fierce competition for places. They can provide a genuine alternative to university for those who want to go straight into work. Even if you get top grades, you shouldn't feel like you 'ought' to go to university; many companies are looking to recruit bright school leavers eager to head straight into the world of work.

Think about your career aspirations...

In all likelihood, your choice will be dictated by your career aspirations. There are still certain careers that you can only really access via a degree. For example, there is no apprenticeship scheme for doctors. If you want to become a doctor, you'll have to do a medicine course at university. However, in other occupations, you'll get the same chances as graduates by completing an Advanced or Higher Apprenticeship scheme. For example, BDO runs a school-leaver programme where the first two years are a higher apprenticeship, and after that the trainees study for the ACA. It takes five years in total to reach chartered accountancy status, whilst it might take a graduate six years.

Money matters...

Money will be another huge point to consider. The boon of an apprenticeship is that the cost of your training is covered by the employer and you are paid whilst you are learning. The much publicised downside to university is the cost: the tuition fees can be hefty and you also have to factor in living costs. There is plenty of financial support in the form of loans, grants and bursaries from the Government to help you cover the cost of university, so everybody, no matter what your financial circumstances, should be able to afford university. However, the fact that you'll be earning a wage whilst receiving training and earning qualifications as an apprentice is a huge advantage.

The disadvantages of apprenticeships...

Of course, you'll also need to weigh up the disadvantages of doing an apprenticeship over going to university. There might be many types of apprenticeship, but not all career paths and industries are covered. Just as university isn't for everyone, apprenticeships aren't for everyone. If you don't have a clear idea of what career you want to enter, studying a traditional subject at university can help you keep your career options open whilst gaining a qualification.

Furthermore, if the apprenticeship does involve a higher qualification, you probably won't get much choice when it comes to choosing a university or course. Also, there's the issue of missing out on the full university experience. Everyone always mentions the social side of university, but you'll also miss out on the experience of devoting yourself to full-time academic study for three years. University can be an unrivalled experience, so it's not something to dismiss lightly.

What's the hurry?

If you're doing A-levels, there's nothing stopping you applying to universities and apprenticeship schemes simultaneously. This means you don't have to narrow down your options straight away; it will give you a bit of breathing space so you can make your decision. Through the application process, you'll be able to find out more about the different universities and companies, and get a better sense of what the university course/apprenticeship will involve. This will help you decide which route you want to pursue.

Remember, it's your choice, so don't feel pressured to go down a particular route because that what's everyone is telling you to do. Take the time to do your research, talk to people who've done an apprenticeship and those who have been to university and consider your own personal motivations.

⇨ The above information is reprinted with kind permission from AllAboutSchoolLeavers. co.uk. Please visit their website for further information.

Lack of jobs and higher tuition fees fuelling surge in young 'Generation Y Not!'

Lack of jobs and higher university tuition fees have led to a growing number of teenagers and young people aspiring to be their own boss, research by PC World Business published today found.

With A-level and GCSE results recently published and a sixth of young people aged 16–24 years classed as NEET (not in education, employment or training), the study found that nearly half (44%) of young people are looking to set up their own business and are using technology to supercharge their business ideas more than ever before.

44 per cent claimed they could run their whole business using just a laptop and Internet connection leading to PC World Business dubbing them the 'Generation Y Not!' entrepreneurs.

'Even though more young people are looking to start a business, the research found that there are barriers to setting up on your own'

Generation Y Not! entrepreneurs

A massive 80% of 16-year-olds have had a business idea for two years or less (some since they were only 14 years old), and with university tuition fees on the rise, they are now ready to set up their firms and become the next Richard Branson.

46 per cent are aiming to set up on their own in the next two years and an ambitious 19 per cent are looking to set up their business in the next six months. Celebrity business programmes, such as The Apprentice and Dragon's Den, are influencing this group of young business stars, with nearly half (49 per cent) claiming they are more aware of entrepreneurial career options after watching business TV programmes.

The research revealed some of the best Generation Y Not! business ideas, which included a device for compressing rubbish so you can fit more into your bin and self-hoovering carpets.

UK search for the best teen business brains

To celebrate this growing trend, PC World Business is launching a competition to find Britain's best Generation Y Not! entrepreneurs, rewarding those with the best business ideas as well as those who use technology in innovative ways.

The competition is one of the first in the UK to ask entrants to Tweet their business plan in 140 characters or less to www.twitter.com/Gen_Y_Not. It opens for entries on 7 September 2011, at the start of the academic year, and the five finalists and ultimate winner will be judged by a panel of the UK's most successful entrepreneurs including Jamie Murray Wells, who founded Glasses Direct while at university and Oliver Bridge, who founded Bigger Feet when he was 15 years old.

Prizes include the latest IT kit, free membership to one of The Office Group's stylish office spaces and exclusive tailor-made mentoring sessions with Jamie Murray Wells, business experts from Dixons Retail, parent company of PC World Business, and M&C Saatchi PR.

The competition closes on 14 October 2011 and judges will be looking for entrepreneurs with a great business idea, have demonstrated an innovative use of technology and have drive, passion and vision to realise their goals.

Phil Birbeck, managing director, PC World Business said: 'By launching the Generation Y Not! competition, we are demonstrating our commitment to helping young business people realise their potential, supporting them through technology to set-up their business and celebrating the best of the UK's young business talent. It is vital that any young entrepreneur gets the right advice first time round, as they can save time and money by ensuring they get the right IT solutions for their business at the outset.'

Barriers to setting up a business

Even though more young people are looking to start a business, the research found that there are barriers to setting up on your own. When asked what is stopping them from setting up their own business, 42% claimed lack of funding was the biggest hurdle and 29% said they did not know where to start. However, they were aware of the resources available to help them with their business, with 40% saying they would use the Internet for advice, followed closely by mum and dad (38%) and the bank (29%).

Jamie Murray Wells, founder of Glasses Direct, and judge on the Generation Y Not! panel said: 'As someone who started a business while at university, I am a big believer in helping those people with the drive, knowledge and business ideas to set up on their own. It is hard work and you need a lot of energy, but competitions like this one can give your business a real kick start. They also provide invaluable advice and support on the things that help you make your business successful, such as technology, to help you on your way.'

'There is help out there for young people but it is just about knowing where to turn to,' added Birbeck. 'Technology offers many businesses the opportunity to stay ahead in a competitive market in a cost-effective way. Small business owners and start ups can get free IT business advice from dedicated experts on the high street and do not have to spend a fortune on expensive technology to set up their business.'

PC World Business provides IT solutions for small to medium businesses through its network of over 200 dedicated business centres. Dedicated account managers are available at over 200 business centres throughout the UK and qualified engineers are at hand over the phone and online.

8 September 2011

⇨ The above information is reprinted with kind permission from Leaving School. Please visit www.leavingshool.co.uk for further information.

The true cost of higher education

Can you afford not to have a degree? Sarah Thomas, a second-year student at Keele University, sizes up the statistics.

The financial website thisismoney.co.uk estimated in 2012 that the average cost of going to university is £53,330, which is an astonishing amount of money. But in comparison to not getting a university education, is a degree more cost effective than at first glance? What is the real cost of not going to university?

In 2011 the Office for National Statistics (ONS) published a report in which they found that, over the last decade, people with degrees earned £12,000 a year more on average than those without a university education Additionally, the ONS found non-graduate salaries peaked at just £19,400 at 34, while graduates went on to earn up to £34,500 at 51. However, this is not the only advantage that degree holders have over their non-graduate counterparts.

A US study also shows that non-graduates have worse job prospects in an already stagnant economy. Georgetown University's Centre on Education and the Workforce published a study in 2012 which revealed that graduates gained 187,000 jobs during the 2007–2012 recession, whereas 5.6 million jobs were lost by those without higher education qualifications during the same time period.

This has repercussions on issues which at first might not seem related. As extraordinary as it sounds, there may be a link between the age a person buys their first home and whether or not they have a university education. In 2012 rightmove.co.uk, one of the UK's largest property websites, claimed that a whopping 69% of prospective first-time buyers were university educated, with an average age of 30 compared to 32 for non-graduates.

Overall, the real cost of not going to university is more far-reaching than just the differences in average earnings. Other things to consider are the ability to put away savings or provide greater contributions to pension schemes. Of course, investing in higher education is not the be all and end all; getting a degree is no guarantee of success. However, the studies that I have found speak for themselves; at the end of the day, while paying more than £50,000 for a degree is shocking, the cost of not having a degree is far higher.

⇨ The above information is reprinted with kind permission from The Money Charity. Please visit http://themoneycharity.org. uk for further information.

Six out of ten sixth formers opting out of university do so because of fee worries

Third of undecided pupils do not understand tuition loan repayment system based on salary levels, research shows.

By Peter Walker

Almost six out of ten sixth formers who have opted to not go straight to university have done so primarily because of worries about fees, according to a study by a commercial arm of *The Guardian*.

The survey of almost 1,700 pupils and students at pre-university level, carried out by the newspaper's audience research department, also found that almost a third of those still undecided about university say they do not understand the system whereby tuition fees of up to £9,000 a year are repaid over a number of years, based on salary levels.

The findings will increase concerns about the potential effects of the new fees and loans system on access to higher education. In August the Independent Commission on Fees said the increase in tuition fees had resulted in a noticeable drop in the number of English students applying for university places during this academic year, with a shortfall of about 15,000 applicants compared with the number that would be expected.

There have also been worries about whether would-be students understand the finance options available to them. Last month the personal finance guru Martin Lewis, who is heading an independent taskforce on student finance information, warned that many were not receiving the proper advice.

The Guardian research, while not a fully representative scientific poll, canvassed the views of almost 1,700 respondents, almost all in England and Wales with a handful in Scotland, using a mixture of a selected panel and responses from schools and colleges, social media and the newspaper's website. The respondents were almost all aged 16 to 21, though there was a bias towards females, who comprised 69% of the sample.

Of those who said they were definitely not planning to attend university or were still deciding, 58% said fees were the main reason to not attend. Of those still making up their minds, 28% said they did not understand the student loans system. The figures need to be treated with a certain amount of caution given the relatively small sample size: only 13% of those questioned were not planning to start university immediately.

Among those who are attending, comprehension of the fees system is significantly better, with only 8% saying they do not understand it. However, almost a third said the level of annual fees – which range this year from around £6,000 to the £9,000 cap – had affected which institution they applied to. Of the same group 4% will be studying abroad, including in Scotland, although almost half said they had considered this option.

Other answers from those planning to attend university reflected the currently straitened economic times: almost nine out of ten felt they would need a degree to get a job, while 80% said they expected to do unpaid placements or internships, whether while at university or afterwards. Almost half, 45%, said even an undergraduate degree might not be enough and that a postgraduate qualification or MBA might be necessary for them to stand out in the jobseekers' crowd.

A Department for Business, Innovation and Skills source said: 'Going to university today depends on ability, not the ability to pay. Our university system is better and fairer than under Labour: most students will not pay upfront to study; there are more loans and bursaries for those from poorer families; applications from disadvantaged backgrounds are holding up; and loans are only repaid once graduates have jobs and are earning over £21,000 – that's 40% higher than under the previous system.'

31 October 2012

⇨ The above information is reprinted with kind permission from *The Guardian*. Please visit www.theguardian.com for further information.

Record number of applicants accepted into UK higher education

The *2013 UCAS End of Cycle Report* paints a picture of increased recruitment at the UK's universities and colleges following a dip in 2012. Some 495,596 students were accepted to full-time undergraduate courses, 6.6 per cent up, and the highest total ever recorded.

Acceptances of UK students to UK institutions are also at a record level (433,612), 6.7 per cent up, with young people and the most disadvantaged more likely to enter higher education than ever before. Most of the increase relates to institutions in England (7.1 per cent) and Wales (5.7 per cent); institutions in Northern Ireland grew by 9.2 per cent and those in Scotland by 1.5 per cent.

'Young people across the UK are more likely to enter higher education than at any time before'

There are a number of key findings from the report.

⇨ Young people across the UK are more likely to enter higher education than at any time before.

⇨ Entry rates for disadvantaged young people are at the highest levels recorded across the UK with disadvantaged 18-year-olds in England 70 per cent more likely to enter higher education in 2013 than in 2004.

⇨ There were substantial rises in the disadvantaged and free school meal entry rate to higher tariff institutions – by 11 per cent and 22 per cent, respectively – but both remain low compared to advantaged groups.

⇨ An increase in 19-year-olds in 2013 pushed the overall entry rates for those who were 18 in 2012 up to 40 per cent, a new high, and redressing the dip in entry for 18-year-olds in 2012.

⇨ Almost all 18-year-old A-level applicants got offers in 2013. Institutions made a record number of offers so that over half of applicants received four or more offers and almost a third had five offers* to choose from.

⇨ Acceptance rates and acceptances for all age groups in the UK have increased in 2013: 76,900 UK 20–24-year-olds were placed in higher education in 2013, an increase of 8.3 per cent and more than in any other cycle.

⇨ More students were placed at their first choice of course, including a 20 per cent rise in the number using Clearing as their first application route.

⇨ At English institutions, where the cap on recruitment was lifted for students with equivalent grades of ABB or better, the proportion of acceptances with these grades fell by one per cent. There were increases in accepted students meeting the ABB threshold through BTEC (vocational qualifications), especially in lower and medium-tariff institutions.

⇨ The most selective institutions accepted ten per cent more students in 2013. They also accepted more students outside the high grade ABB set, 70 per cent higher than two years ago.

Commenting on the report, UCAS Chief Executive Mary Curnock Cook said: 'Predictions of a reduced appetite for higher education following the rise in tuition fees were premature. With 19-year-old admissions up by 18 per cent in England, we can see that the dip in demand in 2012 was perhaps a pause for thought – more of those who were 18 in 2012 have now started university than those who were 18 in either 2010 or 2011.

'Greater competition amongst institutions meant that aspiring students were able to choose from a record number of offers and were more likely than ever to gain a place on their preferred course, including through Clearing, which was a genuine market place for all types of courses and institutions this year.

'The higher education sector has been particularly successful in attracting and enrolling applicants from disadvantaged backgrounds in 2013 and I welcome this further reduction in the gap between rich and poor.'

However, she went on to warn that the UK is still experiencing a decline in the young population. 'The population fall, coupled with a declining proportion of pupils taking A-levels compared to vocational qualifications, is changing the pipeline for recruitment to higher education.'

Notes:

*Applicants can make five choices when they apply through UCAS.

You can learn more about the BTEC qualification by visiting the Pearson website.

19 December 2013

⇨ The above information is reprinted with kind permission from UCAS. Please visit www.ucas.com for further information.

Adjusting to university life

Whether this is your first time away from home or you are going back to study after a break, starting university is a time of great change.

Even if it is exciting, change is not always easy to cope with. The first few days can be quite bewildering with so many meetings, a sea of new faces, things to do and finding your way around the campus.

It is not at all unusual or surprising to feel lost or lonely in this situation. Other new students may be feeling just the same, and this is the ideal time to meet and make friends. It is important to give yourself time when in this transition and not to expect too much of yourself.

The W-curve and the first year of university

Based upon research done with students studying abroad, the W-curve is a predictable pattern of stages which any first-year student can experience after arriving at university.

Initially, you may think you have made a mistake in going to university but knowing about the W-curve helps you see culture shock as part of a journey everyone goes through.

Emotions during the first year of university often follow a W-shaped curve

The honeymoon

The honeymoon starts before students first arrive on campus. Although they may also experience some nervousness, the overall feeling is generally one of excitement and positive anticipation. In Freshers' Week there is generally a strong sense of welcoming from the campus community. The initial sense of freedom new students feel is often exhilarating.

It is common though for students to begin to have some feelings of homesickness mixed in with all of the fun and energy of a new beginning.

Culture shock

As the newness of the college culture begins to wear off, new students begin to deal with the reality of all the adjustments they are going through: sharing living areas, meeting people from different backgrounds and cultures. Routine tasks that were taken for granted at home can become problematic chores. Working out where to shop, get a haircut or receive medical attention can create feelings of insecurity and frustration. The less rigid routine of university can also be unnerving.

Students are becoming self-sufficient, establishing identity, and accepting responsibility for their actions. First-year students have many personal issues to deal with in addition to focusing on academic work: reworking relationships with parents, establishing new relationships with peers, dealing with conflicting values, separation and its resultant anxiety. It is a period of huge, potentially positive change, but also a period of intense personal conflict and anxiety.

Initial adjustment

As initial adjustments are made, new students experience an upswing and sense of well-being having successfully managed issues that have come their way. They fall into a routine as they gain confidence in their ability to handle university life. They feel they have regained control and normality in their lives. Conflicts and challenges may still continue to come

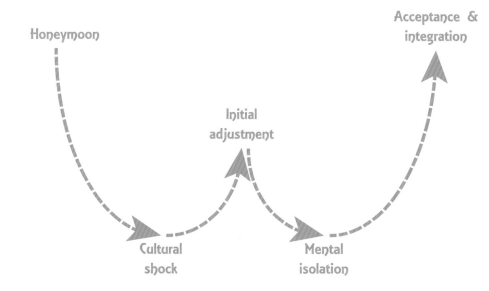

and go, but students are now feeling more in the swing of things.

Mental isolation

When students go home at Christmas they make comparisons between their university culture and their more familiar home culture. Strong feelings of homesickness begin to surface and it is a time of feeling caught between two worlds. University is still not as comfortable as home used to be but home is not as familiar as it once was.

You may not realise how much you miss home until you have been away for quite a while. And even then, going home to visit can still leave you feeling homesick for a home environment that no longer seems to exist. Changes may have happened at home too, and not having been there on a day-to-day basis can be upsetting.

Acceptance, integration and connectedness

As you become more involved in university life, gain some history with new friends and get to know academic expectations, you begin to feel a better connection to the campus community. You begin to have a more balanced and realistic view of the university, seeing and integrating the good experiences with the challenges.

Tips for settling in

Take time for reflection

Build in some time every day to just chill out rather than bouncing from one event to the next constantly. It is important to get enough sleep, but also to relax with music, the paper, in a hot bath or doing whatever you like doing.

Taking time out lets you reflect on your new experiences. You may wish to use it to consider decisions about your course, who to spend time with or what to get involved in.

Expect it to be nerve-racking

Remember everybody is finding their feet, however cool and confident they may appear. You are surrounded by people from different backgrounds and of different nationalities, but the one thing everyone has in common is that they are surrounded by strangers and do not want to be rejected.

Anxiety at this stage is completely normal and if you do not find your lifetime friends in the first fortnight, you are certainly not alone. Having a few nerves does not mean you are going wrong.

Maximise the chances of finding people you get on with

Go to things you know you will enjoy. Do not feel you have to keep in with the crowd at all costs. If you have longed to explore different interests or change

your image, but not had the chance, university is a great opportunity.

Do not beat yourself up

Do not worry if you are not always at ease socially, or if you say or do something you later regret. Learn whatever lesson is there for you, then forget about it and move on.

Do not be pressurised into doing things you do not want to do

Whether it is spending more money than you can afford, using drugs, having sex or even just going out when you are knackered, you do not have to do anything if you do not want to.

Do not bottle up problems

Talk to someone: either a friend, family member or one of the student support teams.

Be organised from the start

University life demands a high level of self-organisation because you have so much freedom. Think about how you divide up your time and get clear how many hours a week of academic work you need to put in. Doing so will help you to make the most of your free time.

⇨ The above information is reprinted with kind permission from The University of York. Please visit www.york. ac.uk for further information.

Homesickness can affect anyone

If you're at university for the first time and feeling homesick, you're certainly not alone. Research shows that 50–70% of new UK students suffer from homesickness to some extent in their first two or three weeks. Most students find their symptoms begin to fade after the third week.

Feeling homesick is not a sign of weakness

Factors that increase your chances of becoming homesick may include being emotionally close to your family, not having spent much time away from home in the past, leaving behind a boyfriend or girlfriend, or not being sure that university is right for you.

Whatever the reason, feeling homesick is not a sign of weakness and there's no reported difference between the sexes in its incidence.

The physical symptoms

Homesickness is a well-documented phenomenon. Physical symptoms range from constant or frequent crying, difficulty sleeping, and changes in appetite, to nausea, dizziness and headaches. Mental symptoms include depression, anxiety and lack of concentration.

Tips for combating homesickness

Make your new room your own by decorating it with familiar things from home.

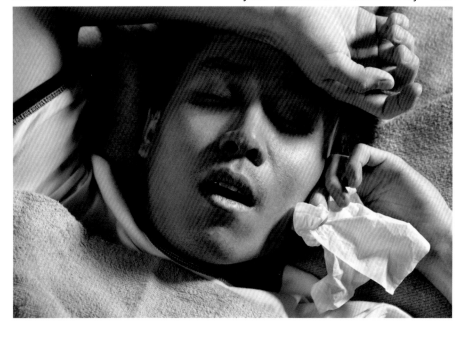

Stay in touch with family

Stay in touch with your folks, but give yourself time to settle in before arranging a visit home, as it may make your homesickness worse. Invite friends and family to visit you instead.

Be realistic

Be realistic about what to expect from university life. Sometimes not everything falls into place at once, but many students go on to have a fantastic time once they adjust.

Join clubs and societies

Get to know people by joining clubs and societies. It's difficult to make the effort when you're feeling down, but making new contacts will help. Keeping busy will help take your mind off your homesickness too.

Sleep well and eat healthy

Make sure you get enough sleep and try to eat a healthy diet. Avoid too much alcohol, as this can have a negative effect on your mood.

Difficulties with your course

If the difficulty of the course has come as a shock, seek help from your academic tutor. They can recommend extra reading or a study skills course to get you back on track.

Consider going to your university counselling service

Most students find their homesickness fades and do not need formal counselling. However, if homesickness is affecting your ability to take part in social or academic activities, consider using your university counselling service.

If you have any thoughts of suicide or self-harm, seek professional help at once.

What to do if nothing works

If you're well into your first year and still feeling homesick and unsettled, you may be thinking you've made a mistake in coming to university.

Don't rush into any decisions about leaving, as things could still improve, but do talk it over with a tutor, student welfare officer, or counsellor.

They'll help you to clarify your feelings and get things in perspective, but they shouldn't put pressure on you to stay at university if it's really not the right place for you.

For a few students, it can be right to leave and take another direction.

⇨ The above information is reprinted with kind permission from the National Union of Students. Please visit www.nus.org.uk for further information.

Spotlight on student security

While you're busy packing all the essentials for university (you know, knives and forks... the odd book...), spare a thought for security...

Leaving home for the first time to go to university can be one of the most exciting and daunting times in life. However, amid the excitement and pandemonium of Freshers' Week, it's important to be aware of personal safety and home security. Student houses and halls of residence attract opportunistic burglars, with a shocking one in five students falling victim to crime, while studying at college or university!

Moving-in day is often a stressful and busy time, but be careful not to leave your room unattended whilst moving in, as the hustle and bustle of bags and boxes can provide the perfect cover for a burglar to strike unnoticed. Statistics from the National Union of Students website show that the average cost of a student break-in is £900 to cover the cost of replacing belongings and repairing damage – a depressing figure if you're strapped for cash and struggling to survive on a student loan.

To avoid burglars getting the better of your home, make sure you close and lock all doors and windows when you're not there – even if you're only popping out for a few minutes. Without mum and dad around to nag about keeping doors and windows locked it's also a good idea to invest in a home safe to keep your valuables secure. Security specialist Yale offers a value safe, which is affordable and comes in various sizes. Another top tip is to avoid notes on your door saying you're away or 'back in half an hour' – instead tell your friends face-to-face so that they can keep an eye on your room while you're not there.

Bicycles are a great way for students to travel; they are cheap, convenient and great exercise, but unfortunately thieves are fond of them too! The best way to protect your bike is to invest in a sturdy bike lock; Yale offers four different types of locks to choose from. For maximum protection, use two locks of different types (a D-lock, robust chain and padlock is ideal). It is also necessary to secure your bike when it is outside your flat or halls of residence, as statistics show almost half of all bicycles are stolen from the owner's dwelling.

Personal safety also needs to be high on the agenda; living away from home in an unknown city can be a scary experience. After evenings out, try to travel home with friends or in a licensed, reputable taxi – remember there is safety in numbers! If you do walk home, try to stick to main roads and footpaths and avoid poorly lit areas – especially shortcuts, such as parks and dingy alleyways. For additional security, why not carry a personal attack alarm? The Yale personal attack alarm is battery operated and has a built in siren and cord loop for convenience. It is simply activated, easy to carry, discreet, and will provide students with additional peace of mind.

⇨ The above information is reprinted with kind permission from The Student Pocket Guide. Please visit www.studentpocketguide.com for further information.

© 2014 The Student Pocket Guide Ltd

Students warned to avoid rent scams

By Simon Thompson

Fraud watchdogs are warning about rent scams as students hunt for homes as universities ready to start the new academic year.

The National Fraud Intelligence Bureau (NFIB) has issued a checklist to reduce the risk of losing cash to fraudsters.

The scams offer housing in prime areas at below market rents and ask for deposits or some payment upfront to secure the property prior to viewing, or to prove the students have the money in order to rent for the duration.

Prospective tenants hand over credit card details, cheques or cash before seeing the property, which turns out to belong to someone else or not to exist.

Payments are then not returned and the student cannot get in contact with the supposed 'landlord'.

Sometimes, fraudsters borrow keys to view properties themselves and pretend to be landlords or letting agents while showing students round.

NFIB is urging students to safeguard themselves by following a rental code:

⇨ Don't send money upfront – Make sure the property exists and anyone you speak to has control of the property. Deposits are standard when renting, but paying money upfront to secure a room is not.

⇨ Protect your deposit – When a deposit is taken other than a 'holding deposit', the money must be paid into a deposit protection.

⇨ Use your common sense – If the rent seems too cheap, then it's probably too good to be true.

⇨ Visit the house you intend to rent – Make sure you visit the property with the landlord to confirm the agreement. Be suspicious if anyone refuses to let you visit the property without paying some money.

⇨ Ask for ID from the landlord – Check the landlord's driving licence or passport to make sure they are who they say they are.

⇨ Ask for evidence that the property exists – Ask to see safety certificates or utility bills.

⇨ Beware of adverts with no telephone numbers or free email services – Look for UK telephone numbers.

⇨ Check the advert – Avoid adverts with no photographs or multiple adverts with the same photographs.

⇨ Be cautious on how you send money – The safest way to pay is by credit card in person at the letting agent's office after a tenancy agreement is signed.

⇨ The above information is reprinted with kind permission from accommodationforstudents. com.

© accommodationforstudents.com

Case study: Kelly, London

'When I first arrived in London, I stayed in a tiny, cramped, B&B while looking for student accommodation. After a few days of searching, and some disastrous viewings, I came across an ad for a great looking house close to the tube, sharing with two other students. I replied to the ad and was told the landlord, Gary, would meet me at the address to show me around and have an informal chat. Gary was great; he made me a coffee, gave me a tour of the house and told me that the other two housemates were female students from the same university as me. He said that the room was in high demand, because of the location and the standard of accommodation, and advised that if I was keen I should sign-up as soon as possible. The house was amazing, it was immaculate and stylish, nothing like the student hovel I'd been expecting to end up in.

The rent was at the top end of my budget, and I hadn't met the other housemates, but I was sure that if I didn't take the opportunity, someone else would, and I couldn't bare the thought of losing out on such an incredible find. So I asked if I could sign the lease on the spot. I wrote Gary a cheque for the first two months' rent in advance, plus damage deposit – a total of £2,000 – and signed a six-month lease. Gary said I should meet him back at the house in a week's time, when he would introduce me to the other housemates and give me my keys etc.

A week later, I arrived back at the house and knocked on the door, suitcases in tow. A middle-aged woman answered. 'I'm here to meet Gary,' I said, 'I'm the new housemate.' The woman had no idea what I was talking about.

After a long and confusing conversation, I realised I had been conned. The woman and her husband owned the house and had been away on holiday for the past three weeks. 'Gary' had broken in to their home, impersonated a landlord, posted a fake ad, and taken £2,000 of my money. Then disappeared into thin air. The police had no way of tracking him, and no way of getting my money back.

In hindsight I feel so naive. I just had no idea that people would go to such extreme lengths to scam someone. My advice to anyone searching for student accommodation is to go through legitimate agencies and be very, very careful when looking at ads online.'

What should you budget for at university?

When I went off to university, I didn't give my weekly budget a second thought. I had my tuition fee loan, my maintenance loan and a nice interest-free overdraft with my new student bank account. So I just turned up and got on with it. Luckily, I was relatively sensible and had parents who helped me out occasionally. However, I had many friends who ate into their overdrafts a frightening amount, struggling to pay them off after graduating.

I graduated six years ago, and graduate jobs are now increasingly hard to come by. Rents are higher, part-time jobs are more difficult to find and it is more important than ever for students to think about their budget before they go to university.

A lot of universities now have budgeting sections on their websites – the University of Nottingham, from which I graduated, has a particularly good budget planner that allows you to plug in all your numbers (from loans to the cost of nights out) and see what's left. But, if you want to draw up a budget yourself, here are some things to consider:

Your income (per month):

⇨ Loans

⇨ Scholarships

⇨ Grants

⇨ Part-time work

⇨ Your own savings

⇨ Contributions from your parents/family

⇨ Other.

Your essential outgoings (per month):

⇨ Accommodation/rent

⇨ Internet (and telephone)

⇨ TV licence

⇨ Gas/electric

⇨ Water

⇨ Food

⇨ Travel

⇨ Medical (dentist, optician, prescriptions, etc.)

⇨ Toiletries.

Living costs and entertainment (per month):

⇨ Mobile phone

⇨ Eating out

⇨ Clothes

⇨ Gym

⇨ Nights out

⇨ Study costs

⇨ Tuition fees

⇨ Books

⇨ Equipment

⇨ Stationary

⇨ Trips

⇨ Other.

Sticking to your budget

When you are calculating your budget, try to be realistic. Think about whether you are the sort of person who is able to be very frugal and strict. Could you allow yourself just £10 a week for food? Or would you cave in and order takeaways? What about socialising? Could you limit yourself to just one night out per week?

If you feel like you will struggle to stick to your budget, try taking out a weekly allowance in cash. This will enable you to physically see how much money you have to play with, and will stop you paying for things on credit cards.

It is very tempting, when your first loan or grant comes through, to give in to the excitement and spend-spend-spend. But remember that you will still want to socialise at the end of term. If you draw up a budget before term starts, you'll be able to relax and enjoy yourself without getting into debt or running out of money.

20 February 2014

Debt-ridden students forced to cut back on food

Students from the UK are on average £16,000 in debt after just one year at medical school, a major BMA survey has revealed.

First years are increasingly using commercial loans and credit cards to plug gaps and more than two thirds reported cutting back on food, heating and other essentials.

One first year, who had taken a degree in another subject before studying medicine, owed a staggering £84,500, and another was working more than 40 hours a week alongside studying in order to make ends meet.

The financial burden is so high that 4.2 per cent of first years were considering leaving their course, according to the survey findings.

Undermining participation

Students in England were particularly hard hit, entering medicine as they did after annual tuition fees rose from £3,290 to £9,000 in the 2012/13 academic year.

In line with BMA predictions, they are likely to owe around £70,000 by the time they graduate – a stark contrast to the final-year medical student debt of £24,000 in 2010/11.

BMA medical students committee joint deputy chair Will Sapwell said: 'These figures do not sit well alongside the Government's mantra of widening participation, with one in 25 students considering quitting their courses due to financial constraints.

'How many more bright applicants are being put off purely because of their financial position?'

Commercial borrowing

The online questionnaire was sent to 5,199 first-year BMA members at the end of May and is the 25th such survey by the association.

Among the 623 eligible students who responded, debt levels averaged £16,167 across the four UK nations.

Mean first-year debt was £17,351 for students who studied in England compared with £11,776 for those who studied in Scotland, where there are no tuition fees for Scottish-domiciled students.

Students studying in Wales had a mean debt of £13,770. Fees for home students are £3,375.

Figures for Northern Ireland, where home student fees are £3,645, were not analysed as the number of respondents was too small.

Respondents from Scotland were least likely to have parents educated to degree level, suggesting the Scottish fee policy widens access to students from less-privileged backgrounds.

Rising credit

The findings also indicated a rise in overdrafts, commercial borrowing and credit card debt compared with previous surveys.

Of the 27.5 per cent of students who reported having at least one credit card, 34 per cent owed money on these in 2012/13 compared with just 16.7 per cent in 2010/11 and this amount had increased to an average of £1,590 from £998.

More than half the respondents (57.5 per cent) were thinking of taking on extra paid work to support their studies – although the majority of respondents believed term-time work impacted on their studies.

In addition, 67.6 per cent said they were cutting back on essentials such as heating, food or professional clothes to economise.

The BMA says

Don't be put off! Although medicine is a relatively expensive course to study because of its length and intensity, it is still very much a realistic and rewarding career for students from all backgrounds. Financial support is available through the NHS Bursary scheme, and for those in difficult financial circumstances all HEIs and many national charitable organisations offer bursaries and awards schemes. For more information about finance for medical students see bma.org.uk/studentfinance.

30 September 2013

⇨ The above information is reprinted with kind permission from the British Medical Association. Please visit www.bma.org.uk for further information.

© BMA 2014

Gender segregation: protests against university guidelines

Students in the UK are demonstrating against university guidelines allegedly backing gender segregation. Channel 4 News looks at what sparked the debate in the UK's biggest universities.

Campaigners are targeting Universities UK (UUK) offices in Tavistock Square, London, after the organisation published a report last month saying universities could segregate by gender during talks from external speakers.

In the report, UUK claimed that universities faced a complex balance of promoting freedom of speech without breaking equality and discrimination laws.

The report presented some hypothetical case studies which come up on campuses, including whether a speaker from an ultra-orthodox religious group requests an audience is segregated by gender.

'Racism of lower expectations'

Chris Moos, a PhD student at the London School of Economics, who is attending the protest, told Channel 4 News: 'What we want to achieve is for Universities UK to immediately rescind their guidelines condoning gender segregation, and issue guidelines that clearly lay out that any kind of segregation, whether under racist, cultural, religious, nationalistic or sexist pretences, is wrong and has no place in the public space.'

Erin Marie Saltman, research project officer at Quilliam and PhD researcher at UCL (University College London), told Channel 4 News: 'This is a bigger issue of racism of lower expectations, of avoidance.

'There is a fear of offending the Muslim community but there are a lot of modern Muslims that would never allow gender segregation.'

In a statement, UUK said: 'The guidance was approved by senior legal counsel as properly reflecting the law. It is not prescriptive. Universities are independent institutions and will make decisions on a case-by-case basis.

'The guidance does not promote gender segregation. It includes a hypothetical case study involving an external speaker talking about his orthodox religious faith who had requested segregated seating areas for men and women.

'The case study considered the facts, the relevant law and the questions that the university should ask, and concluded that if neither women nor men were disadvantaged and a non-segregated seating area also provided, a university could decide it is appropriate to agree to the request.

'It is very hard to see any university agreeing to a request for segregation that was not voluntary and did not have the broad support of those attending. As the guidance explains, there may be many other reasons why a university might refuse a request for segregation.'

'Enforced'

Jo Attwooll, policy adviser at the organisation, added: 'The case studies themselves have been designed around some of the bigger issues that people highlighted.

'In relation to segregation there have been a few publicised cases where segregation has either been requested or has actually happened.

'There was a recent one at UCL where the speaker wanted there to be enforced segregation.

'What that case demonstrated was the need to be clear when you're making external speaker bookings around what the environment will be for that speaker to be given a platform. In that case it only became apparent when the speaker turned up that was what the speaker wanted and the university then took very strong action.'

According to the protest Facebook group, the demo has been organised after 8,000 people signed a petition against the guidelines.

Maryam Namazie, spokesperson of One Law for All and Fitnah, Movement for Women's Liberation, said: 'Today, International Human Rights Day, we rally outside of the office of Universities UK to condemn their endorsement of segregation of the sexes.

'Their new guidance to universities on external speakers states that the segregation of the sexes at universities is not discriminatory as long as both men and women are segregated side by side rather than women being made to sit in the back.

'Would racial apartheid have been non-discriminatory if white and black people had been segregated in the same manner? In fact that is the very argument the apartheid regime of South Africa used when faced with criticism: separate but equal.'

'Widespread'

Earlier this year, a student equality group claimed that preaching by extremists and discrimination through segregation at student events has become a 'widespread' trend at many UK universities.

Student Rights, which carried out the research, found that radical preachers spoke at 180 events at universities including Cardiff and UCL between March 2012 and March 2013.

Segregated seating for men and women was promoted or implied at more than a quarter of the events, at 21 separate institutions.

Among the events highlighted in the Student Rights report was a gender-segregated event at UCL on 9 March.

Segregation policy

The lecture, Islam vs Atheism, was organised by the Islamic Education and Research Academy (IERA), and pitted writer Hamza Tzortzis against Prof. Laurence Krauss in a debate.

The IERA suggested a sexual segregation policy, and it was enforced at the event.

Men and women had separate entrances – although couples were allowed to enter together – and segregated seating. Organisers' security tried to physically remove members of the audience who would not comply, Student Rights said.

A UCL spokesman said that the institution does not permit segregation at meetings and the university has a 'clear policy' of allowing speakers on campus freely, as long as they remain within the law.

The UUK report

The latest UUK report, which builds on its previous guidance on freedom of speech on campus, states that university officials must consider both freedom of speech obligations and discrimination and equality laws when considering such a request.

It says that if officials decide to proceed with an event with segregation, they must consider whether a seating plan would be discriminatory to one gender.

For instance, if women were forced to sit at the back of the room it could prove harder for them to participate in the debate and could be discriminatory for the female attendees.

The report adds: 'Assuming the side-by-side segregated seating arrangement is adopted, there does not appear to be any discrimination on gender grounds merely by imposing segregated seating. Both men and women are being treated equally, as they are both being segregated in the same way.'

But it goes on to say that if side-by-side seating was enforced without offering an alternative non-segregated seating area, it could be deemed as discriminatory against men or women who hold feminist beliefs.

It adds: 'Concerns to accommodate the wishes or beliefs of those opposed to segregation should not result in a religious group being prevented from having a debate in accordance with its belief system.

'Ultimately, if imposing an unsegregated seating area in addition to the segregated areas contravenes the genuinely held religious beliefs of the group hosting the event, or those of the speaker, the institution should be mindful to ensure that the freedom of speech of the religious group or speaker is not curtailed unlawfully.'

10 December 2013

⇨ The above information is reprinted with kind permission from Channel 4 News. Please visit www.channel4.com for further information.

© Channel 4 2014

Top ten weirdest university clubs and societies

By Sophie Warnes

Joining a club or society when you go to university is highly recommended and one of the most fun and rewarding things you can do during your degree. There is something for everyone – really!

The most famous of all the student clubs in the UK is surely the Bullingdon Club at Oxford University – Boris Johnson, George Osborne and David Cameron are all former members. When we heard there was a beekeeping society, we made it our mission to try and find the strangest, wackiest university clubs and societies in the UK. If you like the sound of them, start one at your own university!

KiguSoc @ University of York

In case you missed it, Kigus (Japanese onesies that look like children's animal costumes) are all the rage now. So it's

fitting that someone at the University of York started this club. Their mission statement says: 'we believe there is no occasion or activity that is not improved by a Kigu' – and who could argue with that?

Assassins Society @ Durham University

Assassins Societies are really popular university societies across the world, and in the UK, the Durham University lot reckon they're one of the most active. The idea is you're assigned a target by the Guild, and you have to kill them without being noticed. The club bio says: 'Membership requires skill, cunning and alertness. Some members turn into cool, calm, collected and ruthlessly efficient killing machines, whereas others become jibbering wrecks, torn apart by paranoia, lying awake at night huddled close to their excessive arsenal of destructive weaponry.'

A bit like playing *Assassin's Creed*, we think.

Re-enactment Society @ University of Liverpool

Again, there are several branches of re-enactment societies at universities across the UK so if you're a history buff, you might want to check and see if they have one at your student union. The re-enactment society at the University of Liverpool exists to 'promote and encourage involvement with the UK and European Re-enactment Societies, and bringing to life the Historical ways of life from many different periods of our history'.

The Curry Society @ Leicester University

Leicester has a great reputation for being a brilliant place to grab a curry, so it's fitting that their university should have a curry society. Ash Davies, Curry Society President, said:

'Leicester is frequently rated as the best city in the UK for curry, one of the reasons that tempted me to join the Curry Society. Although it may sound clichéd, joining is also a fantastic opportunity to meet new people – especially during Freshers' Week. We hold regular trips to Indian and Thai restaurants in the Leicester area that specialise in curry, alongside those that serve less common cuisines such as Nepalese.'

The society are planning to hold a 'curry crawl' in 2013. We reckon this one might be the reserve of those with iron stomachs!

Hummus Society @ London School of Economics

This one isn't so much strange as... We didn't realise people were such fans of the stuff! Past events have included a hummus-tasting evening with over 40 types of hummus, a tour-de-force of a middle-eastern kitchen, hummus-making master-class, summer picnic and scrumptious evenings out. They've even had henna painting and shisha.

Society for Gentlemanly Pursuits @ Keele University

Ah, we like the sound of this society! It is apparently 'based upon the mutual interest in the partaking of fine liquors and music of good quality alongside educated discussion'. The group says they cater for a 'plethora of interests, from Classic cinema to Distillery visits.'

Sounds simply charming.

Harry Potter Society @ Cardiff University

Strangely, Harry Potter-themed societies are gathering in popularity in student unions. This group in Cardiff hosts Triwizard Tournaments, socials, assault courses, and of course film screenings and discussions.

Gog Magog Molly @ Cambridge University

Gog Magog Molly was founded in 1996 to perform at the 80th Birthday Party of Cyril Papworth, who lived in Cambridge and collected the local traditional dances. Molly dancing is the East Anglian morris tradition, originally danced every January by disguised plough boys, when the fields were too frozen to plough. The group will be celebrating their 16th birthday this year.

Helen Barnard, a member, said: 'We retain some interpretations of the traditional dances but have drawn on a range of other inspirations, including Harry Potter, a one-way system, a doctoral thesis, local punting hazards, and we even have an Oompa Loompa dance! It's great fun, good exercise, intellectually challenging, and you get to meet fantastic people while keeping an English tradition alive.'

KrakenSoc @ Southampton University

This society is for people who are into steampunk. The aim is to provide a focus point for those who take part in the steampunk culture, and as part of this, the society organises trips to museums and hosts film screenings.

The Pirate Society @ the University of Sussex

Disillusioned by societies which required an element of skill or specific interest, med student Ben Carter founded the group with one thing in mind: fun. Ben Carter and Chris Postle, who run the society, said: 'The Pirate Society started life as all truly great ideas do: over a few tankards of ale in the local tavern. On a dark and stormy night on Sussex campus, six costumed buccaneers assembled in a campus bar, unaware that they were making history.

'Months later, Cap'n Carter led a crew of 80 pirates on our first Freshers' pub crawl. In subsequent years, scavenger hunts, cinema trips and even a "hostile" takeover of the Students' Union have cemented the Pirate Society's place in legend.'

Now, where's all the rum gone?!

6 August 2012

⇨ The above information is reprinted with kind permission from *The Independent*. Please visit www. independent.co.uk for further information.

Is sleep deprivation ruining your university life?

We're all aware of the effects insomnia has on those who suffer from it – a chronic inability to get little or any sleep that can last entire lifetimes, ruining mental and physical health.

Not many people realise, however, that sleep deprivation can be far more subtle, with ill-effects building up over time to cause severe health problems.

The standard advice is to get seven to eight hours of sleep a night; most of us are guilty of getting less than that though!

University students will relate to this all too well. The stereotype of students sleeping all day and studying or drinking all night won't apply to everyone, but it's likely that most students will be staying up late and getting up early for lectures on a regular basis. Along with part-time jobs and nights out throughout the week (particularly during your first year!), there's little chance to establish a good sleeping routine.

It might seem like you're getting enough sleep, but in fact you're simply becoming used to the effects of partial sleep deprivation. Whilst you might assume there's plenty of time to be healthy once you've finished your course, you could actually be sabotaging your efforts to achieve high marks without realising it.

'Sleepiness is a problem at all stages that are relevant to learning, memory and academic performance.' – Derk-Jan Dijk, Director of the Sleep Research Centre at the University of Surrey

Is poor sleep impacting your work?

Sleep deprivation can have negative effects on your motivation, memory and concentration. This means you'll find it harder to attend all of your lectures and seminars, struggle to concentrate on the task at hand, and find it difficult to remember everything you need to know for your work.

If you regularly find it difficult to concentrate during lectures or struggle to complete work you would usually find easy, it could be sleep deprivation taking its toll on your cognitive abilities.

If you're trying to gain work experience or manage to land yourself an internship over summer, you need to make sure you get enough sleep to keep you working at 100%. Lack of sleep can impact on your mood, making you more irritable and depressed – which can give the wrong impression if you're trying to wow a potential employer.

Lack of motivation and focus can ruin your employer's impression of you as well, which might ruin any good references you were expecting for future work.

General health

Poor-quality sleep can impact your physical and mental health in many ways. From depression to obesity and heart attacks, the degree to which sleep affects us is astounding.

There has also been evidence that getting little sleep over an extended period of time can cause depression or anxiety, which in turn can negatively affect sleep even more, causing a vicious cycle.

Your immune system can suffer as well; we've all felt run down and ill after a busy week. Lack of sleep can ruin your immune system and leave you more vulnerable to infection.

Change your sleeping habits

It's easy to reverse the effects of poor sleep if you get into a good routine. Watching TV in bed before you sleep can keep your mind active and prevent you from getting to sleep properly. Falling asleep with the TV or radio on can be particularly bad for sleep, as when the noise changes or stops altogether you're likely to wake up suddenly.

'Not many people realise that sleep deprivation can be subtle, with ill-effects building up over time to cause severe health problems'

It seems obvious but your surroundings can have a large effect on the quality of your sleep, without you realising it. Light sources can affect you even when your eyes are closed – so if you have any alarm clocks or flashing lights in the room at night, it could be worth covering them up when you sleep to see if there's any change.

Colour expert Kate Smith notes that even the type of colour in your bedroom can impact on your sleep 'Whatever the hue, look for colours that have a lower light reflectance value; darker colours have lower light reflectance values than lighter ones and are more conducive to a proper sleeping environment.'

Although it's important that you get enough sleep each night, you shouldn't assume you are sleep deprived if you don't get the full eight hours. Some people may only need six to feel refreshed, while others need far more to keep them going.

However, if you find yourself suffering from any of the symptoms mentioned, you should look at your sleeping habits and think about whether you're getting enough rest for your needs.

⇨ The above information is reprinted with kind permission from Interior Goods Direct. Please visit www.interiorgoodsdirect.com for further information.

The biggest everyday student dilemmas

By Christina Criddle

Maintaining a student lifestyle can be tough; juggling money, mates, sleep and uni can leave you with some difficult decisions.

Even the easiest of decisions are blown up into monumental, life-changing events. Do I get a takeaway or another drink? Should I spend my money on value vodka or fake tan? Do I swipe right to my seminar crush on Tinder?!

Student life revolves around the next student loan and next night out. Yes, students do want to learn but they also want to have fun. When you're paying £9,000 a term, you need to make the most of the free time (ahem, private study time) you're given, as you probably won't get this many free hours again. This can result in every decision becoming an immense pressure and attending lectures can sometimes seem like the biggest dilemma of all.

Most of these #firstworldproblems revolve around money and laziness – two key issues. Students are constantly told decisions at university can profoundly change you as a person, they're part of growing up and character building, and so on. But your most important issues – whether you should wear your killer heels tonight – probably isn't what they meant.

We can all relate to these dilemmas, (who doesn't freak over their poor budgeting skills?) and all have different ways of dealing with them, some descend into a Mariah-esque strop, others silently sob into their textbooks, but it's best to remember how trivial these problems are.

Your mid-lecture 'Costa Coffee is SHUT' crisis may seem like a big deal, but in the wider scheme of things, if dilemmas like these are your biggest issues, you're pretty lucky.

Extending your overdraft or phoning you parents

The tough choice between begging your dad for money, and having to justify how you spent £400 of your loan on an iPad, or extending your overdraft and taking the debt.

Deciding between heating and dinner

You can't be bothered to top up your gas card and there's only £2.50 left on the meter. Do you wrap up in 15 layers and leave the heating off, or just skip cooking supper?

Whether to take your jacket on a night out

The nights are cold, and although you may think booze might numb the feeling, you'll leave the club wanting warmth. Do you take a coat out – stashing it under a seat or carrying it around all night – or brave the bad weather?

Go into uni or 'work from home'

You've got a 9am lecture, which they won't take the register in. It takes you an hour to get to and from uni, and you'll be so knackered from the early lecture that you won't do any more work. Do you stay at home and trust yourself to 'use your time' productively, or go into uni and face doing nothing else for the whole day?

Deciding what film to watch

In one of the few evenings you've chosen not to go out, you fancy watching a film. The problem is, each housemate wants a different one. Do you settle for a lame crowd-pleasing comedy or fight till the death for your film?

Do a wash or buy more pants

You don't really have the time or the energy to do your washing, especially when the likelihood of it drying in a day is slim. Do you wait around for your wash or hop to Primark for some new clothes?

Get the train or the Megabus home

Megabuses are dirt cheap, allowing you to splash your cash on a final night out before the holidays BUT they're usually double the length and the clientelle leave a lot to be desired. Do you tackle the long, potentially smelly Megabus or take an easy ride on the train?

Raid your friend's food cupboard or go to the shop

You're hungover, in your pyjamas and starving. You look in the freezer to find an alluring tub of ice cream. Do you eat it and risk the wrath of your housemate or go out and buy your own?

Take your card out or risk running out of money

You always think you've had a cheap night until you check your bank statement. To avoid this, do you leave your card at home and hope that you'll remember to save enough for a taxi?

Buy dinner or save your money for takeaway on the way home

You will inevitably get a takeaway after your night out but you also want to line your stomach for the night ahead. Do you save yourself for later, skimping on the calories, or tuck-in two times?

Stand in a queue for the women's toilet or sneak into the men's

Nobody can really explain why the female toilets are always busier. Surely the amount of people retouching their makeup, is balanced by the amount of women who go to the loo together in clubs. Queueing can take hours. Do you wait it out or sneak into the boys, hoping nobody will judge?

Deciding which Instagram filter to use

Your selfies from last night need a little 'shoozhing' before they make their public debut – you're faced with a critical decision. Do you use Brannan or Lo-Fi to make your pictures ridiculously cool?

17 March 2014

Survey of 17,000 students finds huge variation in teaching within subjects

In the new high fees environment, do students get value for money? 17,000 student interviews by YouthSight help Which? and the Higher Education Policy Institute answer this important question

Students at some universities study for an average of just 20 hours a week, while others are working for 40 hours or more, new research by Which? and the Higher Education Policy Institute (HEPI), reveals. Their survey, 2013 *Student Academic Experience* was based on interviews with 17,000 full-time students. Fieldwork services including all 17,000 of the interviews conducted were provided by YouthSight via their OpinionPanel Community, the UK's largest youth and student research panel.

Survey findings reveal huge variations in the amount and type of scheduled teaching at UK universities. For example, among students studying maths, contact time varied from 13 to 22 hours per week, depending on the university. One of the study's key findings showed that 29% of students said their course was not good value for money, compared with only 16% the last time this question was asked in 2006 when fees were just over £1,000 a year. The study has previously been run in 2006, 2007 and 2012 with additional smaller waves in interim years. The latest 2013 wave is the largest to date.

17,000 interviews with current students

Undergraduate students enrolled in the 1st, 2nd, 3rd and 4th years of study at UK universities were included in the survey. Fieldwork was completed over three weeks in March 2013 with extensive coverage of the UK student population, including representation of 103 institution and 385 different subjects cases. Engagement with the research was high with many appreciative feedback comments made by the participating students, for example, 'Thanks for asking interesting questions, and the RIGHT questions. Some of them were very relevant personally, and phrased in the right way' and 'Very interesting questionnaire and hope the information helps develop universities and their systems, especially allocating more teaching time to students.'

YouthSight Managing Director, Ben Marks commented, 'we are delighted to have once again provided the fieldwork services for this important research. Our OpinionPanel Community is one of the only research resources in the UK with enough depth of coverage to allow this type of project to take place. I'm particularly pleased with the quality of participation of our student members who really engaged with the questions.'

15 May 2013

⇨ The above information is reprinted with kind permission from student research specialists YouthSight. Please visit www.youthsight.com for further information.

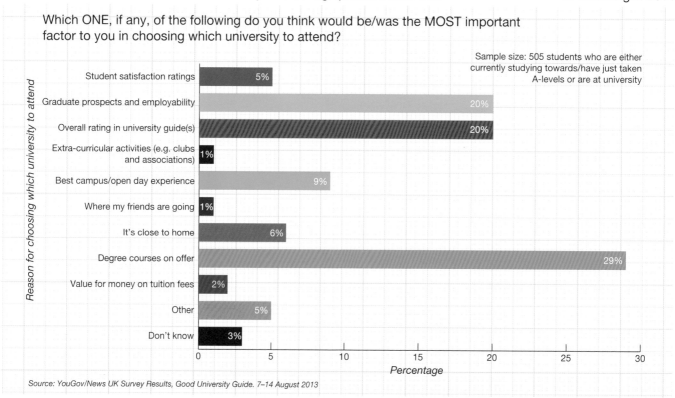

Which ONE, if any, of the following do you think would be/was the MOST important factor to you in choosing which university to attend?

Sample size: 505 students who are either currently studying towards/have just taken A-levels or are at university

Reason for choosing which university to attend

Reason	Percentage
Student satisfaction ratings	5%
Graduate prospects and employability	20%
Overall rating in university guide(s)	20%
Extra-curricular activities (e.g. clubs and associations)	1%
Best campus/open day experience	9%
Where my friends are going	1%
It's close to home	6%
Degree courses on offer	29%
Value for money on tuition fees	2%
Other	5%
Don't know	3%

Percentage

Source: YouGov/News UK Survey Results, Good University Guide. 7–14 August 2013

Student satisfaction at a nine-year high

Students studying at UK higher education institutions (HEIs) and further education colleges (FECs) continue to be very satisfied, with 85 per cent of respondents to this year's National Student Survey (NSS) saying they are satisfied overall with their course. A further seven per cent were neither satisfied nor dissatisfied with their higher education experience, while seven per cent were dissatisfied.

'Students' satisfaction has increased in the areas of Assessment and feedback and Learning resources'

In each of the eight categories covered by the survey, satisfaction has either improved or stayed the same as in 2012. In particular, students' satisfaction has increased in the areas of Assessment and feedback and Learning resources, with an improvement of two per cent in both categories.

Around 304,000 final-year students responded to the survey this year, from 154 HEIs and 165 FECs from across the UK. This represents a response rate of 68.6 per cent, the highest rate in the nine years that the NSS has been running.

The results of the survey, conducted by Ipsos MORI, provide valuable information for prospective students, and help universities and colleges to further improve the education they provide.

HEFCE Chief Executive Sir Alan Langlands said:

'These strong results continue to demonstrate the high-quality student experience provided by universities and colleges in the UK. However, institutions must continue to enhance what they offer and respond effectively to the diverse needs of their students. The NSS provides crucial information which not only informs student choices but also improvements in learning and teaching across the sector.'

Universities Minister, David Willetts said:

'It is very encouraging to see student satisfaction is continuing to rise. University is an enjoyable and life-enhancing experience for most students, as this survey shows.

'The National Student Survey plays an important role in providing students with information to help them make choices about higher education. It also helps universities understand how they can offer students the best experience.'

Professor Janet Beer, Chair of the Higher Education Public Information Steering Group and Vice-Chancellor, Oxford Brookes University, said:

'The National Student Survey has great value as both a reliable source of information for applicants about individual courses and as a touchstone for the benefits of continuing investment in the student experience. It is particularly pleasing to see the increase in the numbers of students participating in the survey and that the improvements in the areas of assessment, feedback and learning resources are being maintained.'

Toni Pearce, National President of the National Union of Students, said:

'It's encouraging to see that the student experience is continuing to improve and that more students than ever have responded to the National Student Survey. The score for assessment is at its highest level ever and we're pleased that the work of institutions and students' unions in this area is showing positive results.

'This is only the second year that students have been asked their views about their union and I'm delighted to see improvement already. Students' unions are a vital part of the student experience and institutions must invest in them if this progress is to continue.'

12 August 2013

⇨ The above information is reprinted with kind permission from the Higher Education Funding Council for England. Please visit www.hefce.aac.uk for further information.

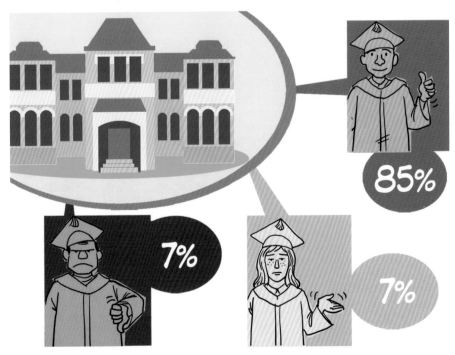

What I wish I'd known before I went to university

Essay writing and internships, socialising and spare time; students and graduates speak to Hannah Fearn about what they wish they'd known before going to university.

An internship is more valuable than a bar job

'I wish I had taken on more unpaid part-time work experience, instead of doing lots of bar work and waitressing,' says University of Manchester graduate and recruitment expert Becky McCarey. 'I needed the money at the time but in the grand scheme of things the £5-an-hour bar work wasn't essential.'

Alice Macris, 23, focused all her attention on her studies in the first year of her law degree at Durham University, but changed tactics in year two. 'I embarked on six internships, after which job offers came flooding in,' she says. 'The more relevant work experience you gain the more attractive you will be to an employer when you graduate,' advises Carl Gilleard, former chief executive of the Association of Graduate Recruiters.

Hone your business acumen outside the lecture halls

Many skills for the workplace aren't taught at university, even on vocational courses. 'I wish I'd known a bit more about life after education. I'm finding it surprisingly difficult to adjust to the real world,' says 21-year-old Vici Royle, who graduated last year with a degree in drama and theatre arts from the University of Birmingham.

Abbie Thoms, a freelance graphic designer now in her thirties, also feels she left university unprepared. 'Finding out how to talk to clients, manage my time efficiently and negotiate finances would have been really useful,' she says.

You'll have a lot of free time – decide how best to make use of it

Physicist, Sarah Kendrew, 32, regrets not taking advantage of more opportunities when she was an undergraduate. 'I was too focused on my course and didn't look around at all the lectures and clubs available,' she admits.

Pete Mercer, vice-president for welfare at the National Union of Students (NUS), suggests societies are the best place to start: 'Whatever your interest, be it Harry Potter, circus skills or curry, there's a society for it somewhere.

If it doesn't exist at your institution simply set it up yourself. You'll meet a lot of like-minded people and gain organisational skills in the process.'

'An overdraft is now a fact of university life, but you should avoid getting deep into consumer debt or being tempted by payday loans'

Don't rush into a relationship

Top among graduate regrets is the attraction of young love. If you're 18 and away from home, it's easy to jump in but it pays to think first.

'For many students, it's the first time you'll have been away from home and this can be extremely exciting and challenging, but also a bit scary,' says Relate counsellor Denise Knowles. 'This makes it easy to form firm or intense new attachments.'

Be prepared to ask questions

Adjusting to the autonomy of university life can be tricky. Detailed feedback and explanations of grades won't be forthcoming unless you meet tutors and ask.

Journalist Liam Kelly, 25, says it took him a term to understand what was expected of him when researching and writing essays. 'In school I was taught that essays had to involve looking at a few theories, whereas lecturers want you to come down on one side of the fence,' he adds.

Students should ask for the support they are paying for. 'It can be difficult to know whether you're working hard enough or are on the right track,' explains Mercer. 'Your course tutors are there to help.' And if you think you have chosen the wrong course, remember that you can change.

Differentiate between good and bad debt

Debt can frighten students and their families. 'I didn't understand the interest rates and as a result I'll still be paying off my debt in 25 years' time,' says 31-year-old personal assistant Emily Poyser.

An overdraft is now a fact of university life, but you should avoid getting deep into consumer debt or being tempted by payday loans. Parents can help by topping up a student loan, but there's no point in paying off your loan early.

'For most people, there's no benefit in paying off student loans as soon as they leave uni. It doesn't affect your credit rating and you only pay it back once you're earning enough,' explains Michael Royce of the Money Advisory Service.

Not everyone is having a ball

Despite appearances, not all students are enjoying the "best years of their life". They may find they miss the parental

Top ten universities in the UK, 2013

Rank 2013	University name
1	Cambridge
2	Oxford
3	London School of Economics
4	Imperial College London
5	Durham
6	St Andrews
7	University College London
8	Warwick
9	Bath
10	Exeter

Source: The Complete University Guide, 2014.

home more than they thought, or that friendships made during Freshers' Week are not as stimulating or enduring as they had hoped. Lowering expectations and allowing more time to adjust can help to put things in perspective.

Guy Roberts, a spokesperson for the Samaritans, says families and friends should look out for signals that new students aren't coping. These include irritability, clumsiness or nervousness; sleeping or eating less than normal; becoming withdrawn and losing interest in their appearance.

University is not the only option

Hannah Thompson, 20, dropped out of her anthropology degree at the London School of Economics earlier this year but was worried her family would disapprove and not offer their support.

'I got myself into a really bad state, trying to stick it out and not disappoint my parents,' she says. 'I knew my dad would take it badly, which upset me, but my mum assured me that my happiness came first and we formulated a rational plan. She directed me to the national careers service and helped me research apprenticeships as an alternative option.'

2 August 2013

⇨ The above information is reprinted with kind permission from *The Telegraph*. Please visit www. telegraph.co.uk for further information.

Student stress

Starting university can be a stressful experience. How you cope with the stress is the key to whether or not it develops into a health problem.

Stress is a natural feeling, designed to help you cope in challenging situations. In small amounts it's good because it pushes you to work hard and do your best. Stress heightens the senses and your reaction times, which means it can enhance your performance, including in exams.

Leaving home to start college means lots of big changes, such as moving to a new area, being separated from friends and family, establishing a new social network, managing on a tight budget and starting your studies.

For most students, these changes are exciting and challenging but, for some, they feel overwhelming and can begin to affect health.

The first signs of stress are:

⇨ irritability

⇨ sleep problems.

Too much stress can lead to physical and psychological problems, such as:

⇨ anxiety (feelings ranging from uneasiness to severe and paralysing panic)

⇨ dry mouth

⇨ churning stomach

⇨ palpitations (pounding heart)

⇨ sweating

⇨ shortness of breath

⇨ depression.

Self-help stress tips

Short periods of stress are normal and can often be resolved by something as simple as completing a task (and thus reducing your workload), or by talking to others and taking time to relax. One or more of the following suggestions might help:

⇨ Assess exactly what in your life is making you anxious. For example, is it exams or money or relationship problems? See if you can change your circumstances to ease the pressure you're under.

⇨ Try to have a more healthy lifestyle. Eat well, get enough sleep, exercise regularly, cut down on alcohol and spend some time socialising as well as working and studying.

⇨ Try not to worry about the future or compare yourself with others.

⇨ Learn to relax. If you have a panic attack or are in a stressful situation, try to focus on something outside yourself, or switch off by watching TV or chatting to someone.

⇨ Relaxation and breathing exercises may help.

⇨ Try to resolve personal problems by talking to a friend, tutor or someone in your family.

Professional help for student stress

Long-term stress and associated anxiety are difficult to resolve by yourself and it's often best for you to seek help. Don't struggle alone. Anxiety can seriously impair your academic performance and that's not only distressing for you, but means a lot of wasted effort.

You may benefit from treatment with prescribed medication or counselling or a combination of both.

Have a chat with your GP or a student counsellor. Student counselling services usually offer short-term counselling and have counsellors that specialise in anxiety linked to exams, workload and other student issues.

14 August 2012

⇨ The above information is reprinted with kind permission from NHS Choices. Please visit www. nhs.uk for further information.

Bullying in halls

For lots of you, your time in halls will have been great, and you will have met lots of people that will remain good friends, and potentially future housemates. However, this isn't the case for everyone, and it's easy to forget that people living near you may not be having such a positive experience. Here's Sam's story.

'I didn't recognise what was happening at the beginning as bullying as such. When I started uni, we had all gone out and socialised during Freshers. It was clear that they were far more interested in partying than I was. At first, this was manageable; we were all settling in and getting used to uni life. Also, there was another flatmate who wasn't much of a drinker, like me. However when she decided to leave her course, it was clear I was on my own.

'As the months passed, my flatmates continued with a "party" lifestyle, and would bring people back to our flat practically every night. After the first or second time that this happened, I approached my flatmates to try to find a compromise. However this just made the situation worse; that night when they got in they began to hammer on my bedroom door shout abuse at me. This continued throughout the year, and during the day they simply ignored me.

'I kept myself to myself after that, avoiding my flatmates and eating in my room. As I had an en-suite room, it was pretty easy to stay out of their way. When house-hunting season came around, I was pretty miserable. Everyone seemed to have someone to live with other than me. I had met a few people through clubs and societies at the Students' Union, but I didn't feel that I knew anyone well enough to ask if I could live with them.

'Luckily, I saw an advert for someone who needed a housemate and the rest is history – that summer I got to move out of the flat and on with enjoying the rest of my time at uni!'

Unfortunately for Sam, she didn't realise at the time that this was bullying, or that there were people who she could talk to for emotional support or to help resolve the situation.

Here are Sam's top tips, should you be in a similar situation:

⇨ Recognise the difference between 'settling in', 'personality clashes' and 'bullying'. Of course the first few weeks will be strange for everyone, but if you begin to feel at any time like you are being singled out, ganged up on, or threatened, it's really important to speak to someone.

⇨ Remember that bullying or harassment is unacceptable, and there are policies in place in unions, universities and colleges to protect students from this kind of thing. Check your student handbook, or accommodation websites to find more information on this.

⇨ Try and speak to your flatmates – they may genuinely not know that they are acting in a way that's unacceptable to you. If they don't respond to this, then it's vital you take the matter further.

⇨ Go and talk to someone in your Students' Union. If the first person you speak to can't help, then try someone else.

⇨ If you are member of a club or society, chat to someone on the committee. They are likely to be a third year, or a finalist, so will know who you should talk to or be able to offer some advice.

⇨ If you are in a situation at the moment where you are unsure of your living arrangements, see if your Students' Union or accommodation office are putting on any housing advice events. These will often have time

for people to meet one another, or lists of people looking for room mates.

Tips if you think someone is being bullied:

⇨ Be friendly, often people being bullied can be really isolated. Talk about day-to-day things; what's been on TV, their course, what they've been up to, rather than focusing on the bullying, unless they want to talk about that.

⇨ Confront the perpetrator.

⇨ Put yourself in their shoes. If you're not sure if it's bullying or banter, put yourself in their shoes and try to imagine how they are feeling.

⇨ The above information is reprinted with kind permission from the National Union of Students. Please visit www.nus.org.uk for further information.

© National Union of Students

Graduates in the UK labour market 2013

Key points

⇨ In 2013 there were 12 million graduates in the UK.

⇨ Steady increase in the number of graduates in the UK over the past decade.

⇨ In April to June 2013 graduates were more likely to be employed than those who left education with qualifications of a lower standard.

⇨ Non-graduates aged 21 to 30 have consistently higher unemployment rates than all other groups.

⇨ Non-graduates aged 21 to 30 have much higher inactivity rates than recent graduates.

⇨ Over 40% of graduates worked in the public administration, education and health industry.

⇨ Graduates were more likely to work in high-skilled posts than non-graduates.

⇨ Annual earnings for graduates reached a higher peak at a later age than the annual earnings for non-graduates.

⇨ In 2013 those graduates that had an undergraduate degree in medicine or dentistry were the most likely to be employed and had the highest average gross annual pay.

⇨ Graduates from the top UK universities earned more than graduates from other UK universities.

⇨ Male graduates were more likely to have a high or upper-middle skill job than female graduates.

⇨ Six in every ten people who lived in Inner London were graduates.

Definition of a graduate

For the purposes of this report the word 'graduates' to refer to those people who have left education with qualifications above A-level standard. This includes those with higher education and those with degrees.

Definition of the population used in the report

The population used in the report is all adults living in the UK who were not enrolled on any educational course on the survey date. The age range focused on is women aged between 21 and 59 and men aged between 21 and 64. The lower age limit of 21 is used as most people will not have been able to complete a graduate level qualification before this age. However, please note also that educational systems are different across the countries of the UK. Upper age limits were used to focus on people active in the labour market. These particular ages were chosen to maintain consistency throughout the report as some sections consider time periods before changes to state pension ages. In 2013 there were 12 million graduates in the UK.

In April to June 2013 there were 31 million people in the UK who were not enrolled on any educational course. Breaking these people down by the highest qualification they held:

⇨ 12.0 million, or 38%, were graduates

⇨ 6.7 million, or 21%, stated that their highest qualification was of an A-level standard

⇨ 6.6 million, or 21%, stated that their highest qualification was

equivalent to an A* to C-grade GCSE

⇨ 3.1 million, or 10%, had 'other' qualifications not categorised in the UK

⇨ 2.9 million, or 9%, had no qualifications.

Steady increase in the number of graduates in the UK over the past decade

The percentage of the population classed as graduates has been rising steadily from 17% in 1992, to 38% in 2013. This reflects changes to education since the 1970s which have led to it becoming more common for people to undertake higher education and less common for people to have no qualifications.

In April to June 2013 graduates were more likely to be employed than those who left education with qualifications of a lower standard.

In April to June 2013 the graduate employment rate stood at 87%, which was higher than the employment rate for those educated to A-level standard (83%), A* to C-grade GCSE standard (76%) and the rates for those with other qualifications (70%) or no qualifications (47%).

Graduates had an unemployment rate of 4%, which was lower than the unemployment rate for those educated to A-level standard (5%), A* to C-grade GCSE standard (8%) and the rates for those with other qualifications (11%) or no qualifications (16%).

The inactivity rate for graduates (the percentage who were out of the labour force, i.e. not employed or unemployed) stood at 9%. This was lower than the percentage for those educated to A-level standard (13%), A* to C-grade GCSE standard (18%) and the percentages for those with other qualifications or no qualifications (22% and 44%, respectively).

Overall, these figures show that in April to June 2013, graduates were more likely to be employed, less likely to be searching for work and much less likely to be out of the labour force than people who left education with lower qualifications or no qualifications.

Focusing on those out of the labour force, graduates were less likely to be out of the labour force to look after the family/home. This is despite the fact that they were slightly more likely to have dependent children than non-graduates (in April to June 2013, 44% of graduates had dependent children compared to 42% of non-graduates).

Different types of graduates and non-graduates, 1992 to 2013

In this section, graduates are split into two groups: graduates who left full-time education more than five years before the survey date and 'recent graduates', i.e. those graduates who left full-time education within five years of the survey date.

Please note that this definition of recent graduates excludes those who recently studied for their higher education on a part-time basis. These are excluded because the report wished to focus on young graduates who have little or no labour market experience. In April to June 2013 the recent graduate group had an average age of 25.

Non-graduates were split into those aged between 21 and 30 and those aged over 30. This was done to create non-graduate groups comparable to the graduate groups in terms of average ages.

Non-graduates aged 21 to 30 have had consistently higher unemployment rates than all other groups

Unemployment rates are related to age. Recent graduates and non-graduates aged 21 to 30 have both had consistently higher unemployment rates than older graduates and older non-graduates. This can be explained by the fact that young people will have been looking for work for a relatively short period of time, will probably lack labour market experience and are not likely to be on a clearly defined career path.

When focusing on recent graduates and non-graduates aged 21 to 30, the recent graduate group had consistently lower unemployment rates. This indicates that going on to higher education can help a young person find a job.

Since the 2008/09 recession, unemployment rates have risen for all groups but the sharpest rise was experienced by non-graduates aged 21 to 30. None of the groups have seen their unemployment rates fall back to their pre-recession levels.

Non-graduates aged 21 to 30 had much higher inactivity rates than recent graduates

Recent graduates have consistently lower inactivity rates than all other groups which may be related to their low average age. However, in April to June 2013, non-graduates aged 21 to 30 had an average age of 26 and recent graduates had an average age of 25. Despite this, 41% of non-graduates aged 21 to 30 had dependent children compared to only 9% of recent graduates. This means a non-graduate aged 21 to 30 was more likely to stay out of the labour force to look after the family or home. This partly explains why non-graduates aged 21 to 30 have consistently higher inactivity rates than recent graduates.

Over 40% of graduates worked in the public administration, education and health industry compared to 22% of non-graduates

In April to June 2013, 41% of all employed graduates in the

UK were working in the public administration, education and health industry. In contrast, only 22% of employed non-graduates were working in this industry.

The public administration, education and health industry is a common one for graduates from various educational backgrounds, which may be due to the wide range of jobs available in this area. It was a particularly common one for those graduates with degrees in medicine/dentistry, education and subjects related to medicine. In fact 92% of those with a medicine degree worked in this industry, 81% of those with degrees in medical-related subjects and 88% of those with degrees in education. This illustrates that graduates with these degrees tend to have a well-defined career path.

Turning to the banking and finance industry, 21% of employed graduates were working in this area compared to 14% of employed non-graduates. However, when considering the distribution, hotels and restaurants industry, the percentage of employed graduates working in this area was below the percentage of employed non-graduates, 10% and 22%, respectively.

Graduates were more likely to work in high-skilled posts than non-graduates

Overall, graduates were much more likely to work in high-skill jobs than non-graduates, but the percentage of each group in upper-middle skill jobs was fairly similar. However, there were significant differences in the types of jobs graduates and non-graduates were doing within this category. Graduates tended to be doing roles in marketing, finance and human resources while non-graduates were mainly working in manual roles such as carpenters and joiners, plumbers and electricians.

Nearly half of employed recent graduates were working in a non-graduate role

Professors Peter Elias and Kate Purcell at the University of Warwick have defined a non-graduate job as one in which the associated tasks do not normally require knowledge and skills developed through higher education to enable them to perform these tasks in a competent manner. Examples of non-graduate jobs include receptionists, sales assistants, many types of factory workers, care workers and home carers.

Using this definition of a non-graduate job and focusing on recent graduates who were employed, the percentage of them who were working in one of these roles has risen from 37% in April to June 2001 to 47% in April to June 2013. Although this time series is variable, an upward trend is evident, particularly since the 2008/09 recession. This may reflect lower demand for graduate skills as well as an increased supply of graduates.

19 November 2013

⇨ The above information is reprinted with kind permission from the Office for National Statistics. Please visit www.ons.gov.uk for further information.

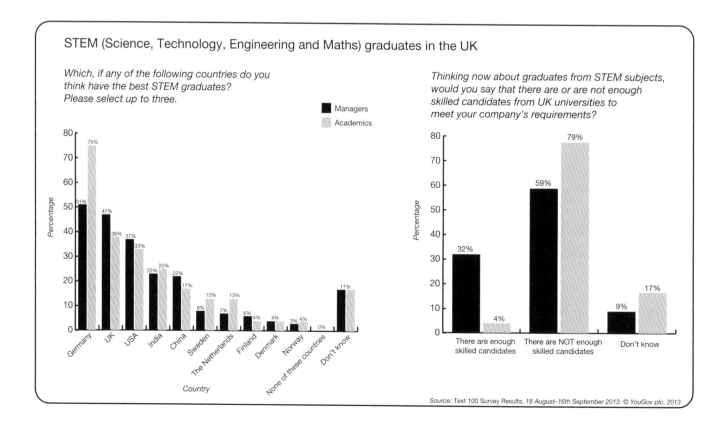

STEM (Science, Technology, Engineering and Maths) graduates in the UK

Which, if any of the following countries do you think have the best STEM graduates? Please select up to three.

Thinking now about graduates from STEM subjects, would you say that there are or are not enough skilled candidates from UK universities to meet your company's requirements?

Source: Text 100 Survey Results, 18 August–16th September 2013. © YouGov plc. 2013

Are graduates shooting themselves in the foot when it comes to getting a job?

The employment landscape is still bleak for thousands of graduates across the country struggling to find a job after years of expensive higher study.

As the aftermath of the recession continues to impact negatively upon the job market, and with fewer jobs available, the competition remains at a high.

Many graduates are beginning to regret their degree choice, sometimes chosen on a whim, minutes before the UCAS application deadline.

According to new research from totaljobs.com, as many as 44% of graduates say they regret not studying something more vocational.

'Degree subjects which prepare individuals for entrance into a particular trade seem appealing to many graduates, who assume that they are a "more effective route to employment",' says Mike Fetters, graduate director of totaljobs.com.

Tanya de Grunwald, founder of graduate jobs blog Graduate Fog and author of *How to get a graduate job in a recession* says her websites' users often attribute their unwise degree choice to school teachers who advised them without 'proper training or expertise to help them make an informed choice'.

When such a large proportion of graduates are unemployed after six months of graduating (nearly 40%), it's not hard to empathise with the unemployed graduate. The independence which students have at university, paired with the control over their situation, quickly becomes a distant reality for many after they graduate.

As de Grunwald says: 'Life after graduation is far from what they expected – as they are jobless, living at home with their parents, skint and losing motivation fast.'

However, it's not all doom and gloom. The recent totaljobs.com barometer data from Q4 2013 showed that graduate and trainee jobs were up by 2%.

Abbie Baisden, Content Editor at Milkround, a popular career source for graduates, told the *Huffington Post UK* the rise in grad jobs is 'very encouraging' but also offered some advice to graduates who have tunnel vision towards grad schemes.

'Competition for any job at the moment is high, and its important that graduates understand that they don't need to necessarily go for grad schemes. Applying for jobs at independent companies can also lead to good graduate jobs.'

Baisden adds: 'What many graduates fail to realise is that having a degree in any subject will have equipped you with many skills, for example in areas such as research, communication and analysis.'

'Many university graduates set themselves a limit on what they can apply for, and have quite a narrow vision of what they can do. Graduates can sometimes have an unawareness of where their skills are useful, and instead stick to a precise target job and fail to see the array of choice at their feet.'

It's well worth digging that bit harder to find information about what other jobs are out there, and tapping into the 'hidden job market' says de Grunwald.

'Build your network, attend industry events and apply speculatively to companies that you read are doing well and expanding. I keep telling graduates to do this, but not enough take my advice. When they do, they say it's a revelation.'

All of the graduate recruitment agencies *HuffPost UK* spoke to confirmed a big no-no for prospective employers is seeing a 'large gap' on an applicant's CV. Graduates can put themselves in good stead by demonstrating that they were proactive in their job search, and worked in the meantime.

Having a degree is undoubtedly an asset, but it's also important to prove to your employer that you have the drive to take control in any given situation.

'Keeping a small job going whilst looking for work looks far better on the CV than a gaping blank space, post-graduation', Baisden told the *Huffington Post*.

Mike Fetters' advice for new grads is: 'Graduates need to prepare themselves for the fact that it may take them a few months longer than they thought to find the job they want… although the job-hunting process can be long, graduate jobs are incredibly rewarding.'

19 February 2014

Unpaid internships: just the job, if your parents can afford it

An article from The Conversation.

THE CONVERSATION

By Kate Purcell, Emeritus Professor, Institute for Employment Research at University of Warwick

The recent news that Westminster School has opted to raise money by auctioning off internships at merchant banks and law firms should come as little surprise. Internships are such a valuable way of getting a foot in the door of a desirable profession that people are prepared to pay hundreds of pounds to give their offspring the chance to work, without pay, at the employer of their choice.

Undergraduate students have two problems not faced by preceding generations: they have to pay for their higher education, and they are expected to leave it with 'employability skills' as well as a degree. This means they often need to work alongside their studies, both to earn money and to gain practical and commercial skills and experience.

The boundaries between employment, work and education have been becoming increasingly blurred, as we found when we tracked a large national cohort of UK students from application in 2005–6 until 2012. Almost four-fifths of the Futuretrack graduates we surveyed between 18 and 32 months after they had completed their courses had some type of work experience during their studies. For 28 per cent of respondents, work experience had been part of their course, either as a sandwich placement or a shorter structured placement.

A quarter had undertaken unpaid work in order to gain career-related experience. But who were those who did unpaid work, and was it worthwhile?

Where are interns working?

The majority of graduates did no unpaid work at all – and of those who did undertake it, most did so during their undergraduate degree only. The subject group with the lowest incidence of unpaid work was mathematical and computer sciences. At the other end of the spectrum, social studies and law, medicine and related, and education had the highest proportions of respondents reporting unpaid work during their degrees.

Graduates from creative arts and design subjects had the highest proportion of respondents who only worked unpaid after graduation. Graduates with interdisciplinary degrees that had included a STEM (science, technology, engineering and maths) subject were less likely to have done unpaid work than those whose courses did not.

In addition to showing differences among the broadly-grouped subjects, our research also found that most unpaid work was done prior to graduation: unpaid graduate internships and work experience are relatively recent developments, not unrelated to the impact of the 2008 recession and subsequent market stagnation.

Focusing on those who had embarked on their courses aged 20 or younger, we found that women were more likely than men to have worked unpaid. There was a strong correlation between socio-economic background and participation in unpaid work. Graduates from professional and managerial backgrounds were most likely to have done so, while those from routine and unskilled backgrounds were least likely.

System favours the better-off

Those with graduate parents, those who had been privately educated and those at universities with the highest entry qualifications – in short, those with the greatest social and educational advantages – were also most likely to have been able to take advantage of unpaid work experience opportunities during their courses and least likely to have worked unpaid after graduation.

These were also the respondents most likely to have reported satisfaction with their current job, their career so far and be most optimistic about their longer-term career prospects.

This raises the equal opportunities issue. It is clear that unpaid career-related experience prior to labour market entry enhances access to professional employment, particularly in those areas of employment where there is an over-supply of qualified candidates. These typically include journalism, the law, arts management and the not-for–profit charity and development sectors, where unpaid and voluntary work have become established as prerequisites to gaining a place on shortlists for paid jobs or training contracts.

Of course, to be able to do such work, it is necessary to have financial support or subsidy, which is where unpaid graduate work has become increasingly controversial because it offers advantages to those graduates whose families can support them through their internships (although Futuretrack also talked to several graduates who were supporting themselves through internships with paid work in other sectors, typically hospitality).

The Government has promoted the introduction of low-paid and subsidised graduate internships to reduce graduate unemployment and skills attrition and to encourage innovation. Since the onset of the recession, more employers beyond 'the usual suspect' industries have become aware of the potential supply of students and graduates willing to work unwaged or for low pay to enhance their CVs.

Opportunity or exploitation?

Unfortunately, it is clear that in some cases they offer internships where there is little likelihood of progression to paid jobs – so that even the relatively fortunate graduates who have been able to accept these have been becoming disillusioned. Concern has been expressed about both the efficacy of unpaid internships in meeting the objectives of the graduates and that such work is exploitative, increasing inequality of opportunity.

Both the Chartered Institute of Personnel and Development (CIPD) and the Association of Graduate Careers Advisory Services (AGCAS) have produced statements attempting to introduce codes of good practice to guide employers in formulating graduate internship agreements. In addition, many universities are refusing to publicise unpaid internships, and a Bill is to be debated in Parliament next year to make the advertising of unpaid internships illegal.

Meanwhile, top public schools such as Westminster are auctioning school-age internships with prestigious 'top employers' to the highest bidders among their pupils' families and the Internet is full of information about 'great graduate internships', many unpaid.

Because they do not constitute employment, these are an invisible part of labour market activity;

in effect, private relationships between employers who are not really employers and the job-seekers who have not found jobs.

Who benefits? Certainly, employers get free work and can 'test-drive' potential employees; some job-seekers gain useful experience and a few of these progress to 'real jobs'. But it is hard to avoid the conclusion that equal opportunities are being eroded.

3 June 2013

⇨ The above information is reprinted with kind permission from The Conversation Trust (UK). Please visit www.theconversation.com for further information.

© *2010-2014 The Conversation Trust (UK)*

Students expect to apply for 24 jobs to land a position

By Andrew Farmer

The economy may be improving but students expect to have to fill out an average of 24 job applications before landing a job, new research from YouGov shows.

As the new university year begins, the "School Leavers and Students' First Jobs" report reveals the expectations for life after lectures of those in further and higher education. It finds that while those at university think they will have to apply for 26 jobs before they find employment, current sixth form students who plan to enter higher education are more optimistic, expecting to fill out 17 applications.

The report shows that sixth form students are also more optimistic about their earning power after graduation, believing they will take home more (£23,000) than those currently studying for degrees (£20,250) when they get their first job after university.

YouGov's research finds that many young people realise the importance of workplace experience when entering the job market. Almost two thirds (64%) of school leavers think that not having relevant work experience could hamper their prospects of working in their preferred career and more than three quarters (76%) of degree students believe it might be a barrier.

The research shows that young people think internships are an important way of deciding on a career. More than eight in ten (85%) of those questioned know what an internship is and among this group almost nine in ten (88%) believe they are a good way to make contacts that can help them find a permanent job. However, there is also cynicism among this group about the practice, with almost seven in ten (69%) thinking that some companies use internships as a way of getting cheap or free labour.

James McCoy, Research Director at YouGov, says: "Although the economy is showing signs of recovery, young people feel that they face an extremely tough employment situation. Most see finding employment as hard work, and the number of applications they expect to fill out is testament to that. They also appreciate how competitive the market is and how much of a premium employers put on experience when hiring staff and on balance feel that internships – although potentially exploitative – are good for their job prospects."

24 October 2013

⇨ The above information is reprinted with kind permission from YouGov. Please visit www.yougov.co.uk for further information.

© *YouGov plc 2014*

Volunteer placements, rights and expenses

1. Find volunteer placements

Find volunteering opportunities on:

⇨ the Do-it website

⇨ in local communities through Community Service Volunteers or on local notice boards (e.g. in a library) or local newspapers

⇨ the VSO website (for overseas placements)

⇨ by contacting a local Volunteer Centre

⇨ the Reach website for volunteers with specific skills – like accountancy, marketing, law, management, mentoring or IT

⇨ volunteer opportunities for people aged 50 or older

⇨ the Volunteering Wales website

⇨ the Volunteer Scotland website.

Young people

Register for volunteer placements at:

⇨ the National Citizen Service website, if you're 16 to 17 in England or Wales, or 15 to 16 in Northern Ireland

⇨ the International Citizen Service website, if you're 18 to 25 and want to volunteer abroad.

2. Volunteers' rights

You don't have a contract of employment as a volunteer, so you don't have the same rights as an employee or worker.

You will usually be given a volunteer agreement that explains:

⇨ the level of supervision and support you'll get

⇨ what training you'll get

⇨ whether you're covered under the organisation's employer or public liability insurance

⇨ health and safety issues

⇨ any expenses the organisation will cover.

The volunteer agreement isn't compulsory, but sets out what you can expect from the organisation you're volunteering for. It doesn't form a contract between you and the organisation.

3. When you can volunteer

Age limits

There's no upper age limit on volunteering. However, some organisations' insurance policies don't cover you if you're under 16 or over a certain age (usually 80).

You can't work for a profit-making organisation if you're under 14, even if you're not paid.

Your local councils might have extra rules about the work you can do as a young person. For example, you might not be able to volunteer at a charity shop if the council decides that it is a profit-making organisation.

People aged 50 or older can find volunteering opportunities with the Retired and Senior Volunteering Programme.

Volunteering and benefits

You can volunteer and claim benefits if:

⇨ the only money you get from volunteering is to cover expenses, like travel costs

⇨ you continue to meet the conditions of the benefit you get.

Criminal records

You can still volunteer in most roles if you have a criminal record, depending on your offences. You might need a Disclosure and Barring Service check if you want to volunteer with children or vulnerable adults.

4. Pay and expenses

You aren't paid for your time as a volunteer, but you may get money to cover expenses. This is usually limited to food, drink, travel or any equipment you need to buy.

You might be classed as an employee or worker rather than a volunteer if you get any other payment, reward or benefit in kind. This includes any promise of a contract or paid work in the future.

You get certain employment rights if you're classed as an employee or worker, like getting the minimum wage.

Example 1

Ellie volunteers at a company to get some work experience. She's given travel expenses even though she walks to work. This is payment, rather than out-of-pocket expenses, so she must be paid at least the minimum wage.

Example 2

Dave volunteers for an organisation tending local parks. All volunteers get £3 a week for travel but Dave is responsible for a park close to his home, so he walks there. This means the £3 is a payment and not a reimbursement of expenses. It could count as a contract of employment meaning Dave could be eligible for the minimum wage.

Example 3

Joe is an unpaid intern at a record company, but he's given free CDs as a perk. The CDs are 'benefits in kind'. They mean he must be paid at least the minimum wage.

Example 4

Amanda is an unpaid intern at a design company. She's been promised that she'll be taken on as an employee after three months. This counts as a reward, so she must be paid at least the minimum wage for the whole time she spends at the company.

⇨ The above information is reprinted with kind permission from GOV. UK.

WHAT HAPPENS TO THOSE WHO DO FURTHER STUDY?

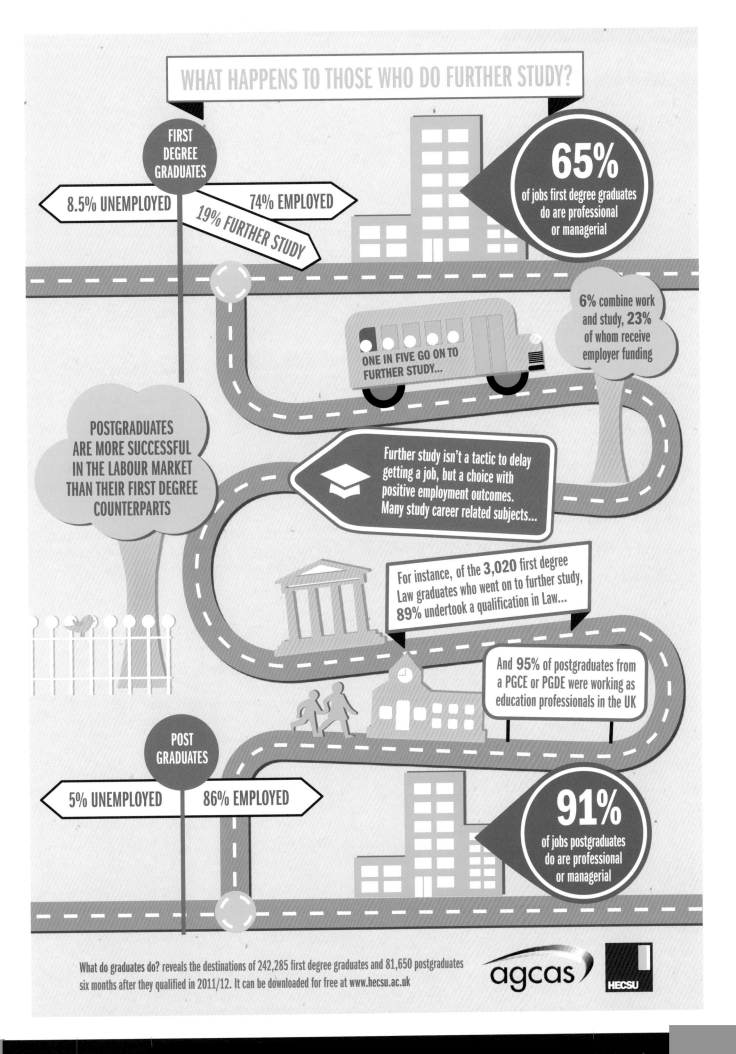

FIRST DEGREE GRADUATES

8.5% UNEMPLOYED

74% EMPLOYED

19% FURTHER STUDY

65% of jobs first degree graduates do are professional or managerial

6% combine work and study, **23%** of whom receive employer funding

ONE IN FIVE GO ON TO FURTHER STUDY...

POSTGRADUATES ARE MORE SUCCESSFUL IN THE LABOUR MARKET THAN THEIR FIRST DEGREE COUNTERPARTS

Further study isn't a tactic to delay getting a job, but a choice with positive employment outcomes. Many study career related subjects...

For instance, of the **3,020** first degree Law graduates who went on to further study, **89%** undertook a qualification in Law...

And **95%** of postgraduates from a PGCE or PGDE were working as education professionals in the UK

POST GRADUATES

5% UNEMPLOYED

86% EMPLOYED

91% of jobs postgraduates do are professional or managerial

What do graduates do? reveals the destinations of 242,285 first degree graduates and 81,650 postgraduates six months after they qualified in 2011/12. It can be downloaded for free at www.hecsu.ac.uk

agcas

HECSU

ISSUES: Stude   ter unive

Key facts

- 56% of people believe that A-levels have got easier, 32% believe they have stayed about the same and 12% believe they have got harder. (page 2)

- 21% of people think it would be wrong to introduce tougher marking rules because it would put current pupils at a disadvantage to previous pupils. (page 2)

- The first Career College will open in September 2014, with an expected 40 more to open in the next four years. (page 7)

- 44% of young people who aren't in education, employment or training are looking to set up their own business. (page 10)

- 80% of 16-year-olds have had a business idea of two years or less. (page 10)

- 42% of young people said that lack of funding was the biggest hurdle in setting up their own business. (page 10)

- The financial website thisismoney.co.uk estimated that in 2012 the average cost of going to university is £53,330. (page 11)

- The ONS found that non-graduate salaries peak at £19,400 at 34-years-old, which graduates earn up to £34,500 at 51. (page 11)

- Research conducted by *The Guardian* found that, of those not planning to attend university or still deciding, 58% said fees were the main reason not to attend. (page 12)

- Research conducted by *The Guardian* found that 8% of people who had decided to attend university did not understand tuition fees. (page 12)

- In 2013, 495,596 students were accepted to full time undergraduate courses, which is the highest ever recorded. (page 13)

- The most selective UK institutions accepted 10 per cent more students in 2013. (page 13)

- The average cost of a student break-in is £900 to cover the cost of replacing belongings and repairing damage. (page 17)

- Students from the UK are on average £16,000 in debt after just one year at medical school. (page 20)

- The Higher Education Policy Institute's 2013 survey indicated that 29% of students said their course was not good value for money. (page 26)

- 20% of respondents to a YouGov survey in 2013 said that graduate prospects and employability was the most influential factor when choosing which university to attend. (page 26)

- In 2013 there were 12 million graduates in the UK. (page 32)

- In April to June 2013, graduates were more likely to be employed than those who left education with qualifications of a lower standard. (page 32)

- Over 40% of graduates worked in the public administration, education and health industry. (page 32)

- The percentage of the population classed as graduates has been rising steadily from 17% in 1992 to 38% in 2013. (page 32)

- In April to June 2013, the graduate employment rate stood at 87% which was higher that the rate for those educated to A-level standard (83%). (page 32)

- Non-graduates aged 21 to 30 have had consistently higher unemployment rates than all other groups. (page 33)

- Six months after they graduated in 2011/12, 86% of postgraduates were employed in 2013 and 5% were unemployed. (page 39)

A-levels

These are qualifications usually taken by students aged 16 to 18 at schools and sixth-form colleges, although they can be taken at any time by school leavers at local colleges or through distance learning. They provide an accepted route to degree courses and university and usually take two years to complete.

Apprenticeship

An apprenticeship involves learning as you earn money. An apprentice will be paid a salary and work towards their desired qualifications. Most apprenticeships take between one and four years to complete and are available in a wide range of industries.

Career College

Career Colleges are schools designed to provide vocational education. This means that students will learn and develop skills necessary to perform particular jobs.

Degree

An honours degree is the most common qualification awarded on graduation from university. It is graded according to classification: first class (a 'first'), upper second class (2:1), lower second class (2:2), third class (a 'third') and fail.

Further education (FE)

Post-16 education, usually provided by a sixth form or FE college offering A-levels and vocational courses.

Gap year

A year away from study or full-time employment, usually taken before starting university or after graduating. Gap years can help students to broaden their horizons through travel or volunteering.

Graduate

Someone who has studied for and been awarded a degree.

Halls of residence

Most new students live in accommodation provided by the university, called halls of residence.

Higher education (HE)

Post-18 education, usually provided by a university and leading to the award of a degree or postgraduate qualification. There are currently over two million higher education students in the UK.

Postgraduate

A postgraduate is a student who has completed a degree and gone on to further academic study, such as a PhD or a Masters course.

State school

A school which is funded and run by the Government, at no cost to the pupils. An independent school, on the other hand, is one which is privately run and which pupils pay a fee to attend. These are sometimes known as 'private schools' or 'public schools' (please note, not all private schools are public schools).

Student debt

A higher education student can apply for a student loan from the Government, which they begin paying back monthly after graduation once they are earning a certain salary. They may also incur additional debts such as overdrafts while at university.

Undergraduate

An undergraduate is a term applied to a student studying towards a first degree but who has not yet graduated.

Vocational

A qualification which is relevant to a particular career and can be expected to provide a route into that career. Examples are qualifications in accountancy or journalism. This differs from an academic qualification, which focuses on a particular academic subject such as History or Maths.

Assignments

Brainstorm

⇨ In small groups, discuss what you know about student choices in today's society. Consider the following points:

- What are the current options for A-level students, besides going to university?

- What are the benefits of going to university?

- Why might students decide *not* to go to university?

Research

⇨ Do some research into different types of apprenticeship schemes in your local area and write a blog post exploring your findings.

⇨ Research the financial help available to students starting university in September 2014. Write some notes and share with your class.

⇨ Read the article *Debt-ridden students forced to cut back on food* and do some research to find out how students could save money and still eat healthily. Create a small booklet that includes advice and recipes.

⇨ Research graduate jobs in your local area and feedback to your class. What kind of jobs are available?

⇨ Choose a subject you might consider studying at university and do some research to find out which institution in the UK is best for your chosen course. Write some notes and feedback to the rest of your class.

⇨ Conduct a survey to find out about your peer group's feelings towards studying at university. Write a report featuring tables and graphs to illustrate your findings.

Oral

⇨ The article on page one, *What can I do with my A-levels?*, lists five different options that A-level students might choose to pursue after their exams. Select one of these options and create a five-minute presentation that explains and explores its benefits. You should also do some research and find some sources that students can turn to for further information on your chosen option.

⇨ In pairs, role play a situation in which a young person goes to their school's careers advisor for help deciding what they want to do after their A-levels. Take it in turns to play the role of the student and the careers advisor.

⇨ In small groups, deliver a presentation to the rest of your class, giving tips and advice about student safety.

⇨ In small groups, discuss the kind of things you would need on your CV in order to be successful in the graduate job market.

Design

⇨ Create an advice booklet for students who did not achieve the grades they hoped for at A-level.

⇨ In small groups, imagine that you have decided to start your own business instead of going to university or doing A-levels. Think of an idea for your business, give it a name and create a plan that explains your concept. You should also create a logo for your business.

⇨ Design an app that will help students deal with the challenges and stresses that might experience at university.

⇨ Read the article *Top ten weirdest university clubs and societies* and create your own university society.

Reading/Writing

⇨ Read the article *Careers guidance services are failing young people* on page four and write a letter to your head teacher explaining what you think careers guidance at school should be like.

⇨ Write a blog post from the perspective of a student who is in their first term of university. Think about the challenges you might be facing as well as the positive aspects.

⇨ Read the article *What should you budget for at university?* And use the bullet point lists to create your own budget.

⇨ Read the article *Twelve of the biggest everyday student dilemmas* and choose one of the dilemmas. Imagine you have received an e-mail from a friend who is asking for your advice on this dilemma and construct a reply.

Acknowledgements

The publisher is grateful for permission to reproduce the material in this book. While every care has been taken to trace and acknowledge copyright, the publisher tenders its apology for any accidental infringement or where copyright has proved untraceable. The publisher would be pleased to come to a suitable arrangement in any such case with the rightful owner.

Images

Cover, page iii and page 12: iStock, page 5 © Craig Garner, page 8: MorgueFile, page 11 © iStock, page 12 © iStock, page 16 © iStock, page 17 © iStock, page 19: MorgueFile, page 28: iStock, page 30: SXC, page 31: MorgueFile. Page 33: MorgueFile.

The infographic on page 39 is included with the permission of AGCAS and HECSU. For the latest version of What do graduates do?, see www.hescu.ac.uk or www.agcas.org.uk. For permission to reproduce, contact wdgd@hescu.ac.uk.

Illustrations

Don Hatcher: pages 1 & 20. Simon Kneebone: pages 4 & 15. Angelo Madrid: pages 23 & 27.

Additional acknowledgements

Editorial on behalf of Independence Educational Publishers by Cara Acred.

With thanks to the Independence team: Mary Chapman, Sandra Dennis, Christina Hughes, Jackie Staines and Jan Sunderland.

Cara Acred

Cambridge

May 2014